For everything
there is a season,
and a time for every matter
under heaven.

ECCLESIASTES 3:1

Blessings on your family journey.
With Joy,
Janie Y. Cook

THE
TOPICAL FAMILY BIBLE COMPANION

- 15 minutes a day
- Appropriate for all ages
- Suggestions for family activities
- Topics covering real family issues
- With special holiday studies

Janice Y. Cook

INTERVARSITY PRESS
DOWNERS GROVE, ILLINOIS 60515

InterVarsity Press® is the book-publishing division of InterVarsity Christian Fellowship®, a student movement active on campus at hundreds of universities, colleges and schools of nursing in the United States of America, and a member movement of the International Fellowship of Evangelical Students. For information about local and regional activities, write Public Relations Dept., InterVarsity Christian Fellowship, 6400 Schroeder Rd., P.O. Box 7895, Madison, WI 53707-7895.

All Scripture quotations, unless otherwise indicated, are taken from the New Revised Standard Version of the Bible, copyright 1989 by the Division of Christian Education of the National Council of Churches of Christ in the U.S.A., and are used by permission.

Family activies: Beth Whittier

Cover illustration: Donna Nelson
ISBN 0-8308-1172-9

Printed in the United States of America ∞

Library of Congress Cataloging-in-Publication Data

Cook, Janice Y.
    The topical family Bible companion/Janice Y. Cook; with
activities by Beth Whittier.
        p.   cm.
    ISBN 0-8308-1172-9
    1. Bible—Children's use.   2. Family—Religious life.
I. Whittier, Beth.   II. Title.
BS618.C66   1994
220.3—dc20   94-27013
                                                                    CIP

15	14	13	12	11	10	9	8	7	6	5	4	3	2	1
06	05	04	03	02	01	00	99	98	97	96	95	94		

To my parents,
Jack and Florence Smith,
and my sister,
Sharlet Wagner.
Ordinary people
living extraordinary lives.

And to my circle of sisters.
In your presence
I have been sustained by comfort,
courage, wisdom and laughter:
Kathy Thompson, Mary Elva Smith,
Kathie Baldwin, Barb LeFevre,
Janine Strautman, Jane Parker,
Patti Hunter, Jackie Williams,
Joan Leeger, Cherylee Duncan,
Sherri Leidecker, Beverly Cleland,
Cathy Bodell, Becky Bates,
Wanda Cook, Cindy Wright,
Kathy Comina, Jan LaBar,
Wendy Fish and Marcia Jourdane.

Welcome to the *Topical Family Bible Companion*

Every day the routine threads of our lives are woven into a holy fabric. The ordinary becomes quite extraordinary, the mundane becomes mystery because God is the source of our lives and has chosen to set us apart. We are invited to see the world through the eyes of a child—with innocence and expectation. At our best we recognize God's imagination and celebrate this glorious adventure that we call life.

The Scriptures speak to us in every season of our lives. Bible characters lend us wisdom, insight and a connection with real things happening to real people. We are able to find our own stories of faith through the faith stories of others. The Bible is *our* story. The character of God is revealed to us and we are called into the presence of the One who knew us before the world began.

We have been given a tool by which to study God's relationship with humanity throughout the ages. What an unbelievable act of generosity. As you study the Scriptures and experience the awakening of your deepest desire to know God, listen intently to one another, care for each other and have fun exploring together all the possibilities.

With joy,
Janice Y. Cook

How to Use the
Topical Family Bible Companion

The goal of this book is to introduce people of all ages to the rewards of daily Bible study. I hope these studies will be enabling tools in placing the guidance, leadership and responsibility for the spiritual awakening and development of children in the loving hands of family.

What Is This Book?
The *Topical Family Bible Companion* is:
1. A home Bible study program designed for parents and children six to twelve years of age.
2. A fifty-two-week topical study of the Bible.
3. Designed so that study can be done six days a week in as little as ten minutes each day.
4. A topical reflection for parents followed by a brief reflection for the entire family.
5. A passage of Scripture followed by two questions. The first

question focuses on the content of the passage and encourages your family to dig into the Scriptures. The second question is meant to stimulate a dialogue between family members which helps them to apply and relate Scripture to their everyday life.
6. Designed to accommodate a broad spectrum of ages. Because the questions are very general, it is impossible to be age-appropriate for everyone. I encourage you to be creative in adapting this program for your children.

How Do I Lead My Family in the Studies?
1. Try to find a regular time each day and allow at least ten minutes to work on your Bible study. Commit your family to that time and make every effort to keep that commitment. But recognize that you'll need to be flexible. Some suggestions on creatively using the Bible study are:
□ As the family gathers for a meal, read the family reflections and the Bible passage, and use the questions to stimulate meaningful mealtime dialogue.
□ Time spent traveling with your family, whether a short distance to school and work or longer trips, can be a great opportunity for a family to do the studies.
□ For a special focus time with one child, use the Bible study with your children individually. This can also be done when time does not permit the entire family to be together.
2. To record your family's progress, date each week of completed study on the chart at the front. You might also want to include the names of family members who participate. Family members will be encouraged by these names and dates.
3. Use a translation that is easy for everyone to understand. The *New International Version, Today's English Version* and the *New Revised Standard Version* are all recommended.
4. Familiarize yourself with the topics included in the book. Be

flexible in choosing the topics to study. Use topics that are relevant to the issues your family is wrestling to understand.

5. Memory work can be a source of encouragement and comfort. Choose a verse from one of the readings for the week to memorize. Some suggestions on how to learn the verses are:

☐ Keep the memory verse posted on your refrigerator at the beginning of the week.

☐ Write the memory verse on an index card, and keep it in the car to learn during travel time.

☐ Encourage your family members to learn the verse through an activity. One way to do this is with a memory puzzle. Write the memory verse in large letters on a sheet of paper. Cut the paper into puzzle pieces, mix them up and time your family to see how fast they can put the puzzle back together.

☐ Keep a daily record of who can say the verse by memory.

☐ The memory verse can be used to enrich your family devotion and prayer life. Use it at mealtime, bedtime and any time you want.

6. Effort should be made to give all family members with reading ability the opportunity to read aloud from the Bible. This can be done by sentences, verses or whole passages. Try not to be too concerned with exact pronunciation, but rather focus on the content of the Scriptures.

7. Sharing and modeling are important aspects of the Christian life and are equally important when using the *Topical Family Bible Companion.* Children and parents alike will be enriched by the open participation of all family members. Sometimes it is helpful for the parents to begin the sharing process. Honest communication can lead to fantastic discussions!

8. Close your studies in prayer. Recognize that each person has a unique style of communicating with God and must develop his or her confidence in praying aloud. Through the course of the study, encourage different family members to lead in prayer. When time permits, group prayer is an enriching experience. Allow each family member an opportunity to pray, respecting those who would rather be silent.

9. There are special family activities throughout the book that are meant to strengthen the point of that week's Scripture focus. The instructions are general, allowing you to use these ideas as you wish. Take advantage of these to enhance family learning and fellowship.

Is This Appropriate for My Child's Age?

The *Topical Family Bible Companion* is designed to be especially effective for home Bible study for children six to twelve years old when used creatively and with some understanding of the developmental personality of your children. I hope the following information will aid you in that understanding.

Primary-Age Children (6-8 years)

Primary school children are open to learning about God and accept almost everything they are told or exposed to about him. Even though they are not able to think logically or express their feelings about God, they are able to talk with God easily if encouraged by their family. They are beginning to read and can recognize familiar Bible verses.

The second question each day, which focuses on personal application, will have particular significance at this age because children live in the present and have little sense of time.

Middler-Age Children (8-10 years)

Middler children are beginning to formulate questions about Christianity. They enjoy participating in worship and are familiar with Bible verses. The children are open to learn about

God and have developed a sense of right and wrong in attitudes and actions toward others. At this age, it is important to strengthen their self-image as children of God who are loved by God.

This can be an exciting time for your family to study together because middler-age children would rather participate than watch. They have also developed an ability to reason and discuss, and are very curious, asking many questions. Additionally, children at this age have a lengthening attention span and good memories.

Junior-Age Children (10-12 years)
Junior-age children question and evaluate different points of view in search of their own convictions and are growing in faith as their concepts mature. They can sense the relevance of the Bible to their decisions and behavior. At this age they understand historical relationships and their significance for the Christian faith. They have developed their ability to think, reason and solve problems and the ability to express religious thoughts.

Steps for Daily Study
1. Read the adult reflection before doing the study.
2. Pray that God may bless your understanding of the Scriptures. Encourage taking turns praying.
3. Read the family reflection section aloud.
4. Read the Bible passage aloud. Parents and children who are readers may share in the reading responsibilities.
5. Read question one aloud. This will help give you a focus for that passage. Have your children answer the questions first to see what their understanding is. This will help give insight to your children's perspective and clarify any misconceptions. Parents, be sure to answer the question also.

6. Use question two to stimulate more personal dialogue.

7. Use the space in the table of contents to keep a record of the date you complete each study.

8. Close with prayer.

Using the "Celebrating the Seasons" Section

Certain seasons inspire and encourage us to pause in reflection, meditation and worship. Even though some have become very commercial, the believer can use the hype as heightened awareness and deliver a whole new meaning to an otherwise hollow celebration.

These seasons serve also as powerful "teaching moments" for adults and children alike. In such times conversations naturally flow into issues of deeper significance. The chance to tell the Christmas story brings our belief traditions into our living rooms. Easter becomes a festival of miracles and new life as we celebrate the resurrection of Jesus. At Thanksgiving in the United States, the pumpkins and turkey turn our hearts toward God in wonder and gratitude as we gather family and friends to share in the feast.

Christmas, Easter and Thanksgiving are familiar holidays. Another season, however, is so significant to us as Christians that we must give it our attention even if the card companies don't! That is the season of the birth of the church—Pentecost. In a confusing and frightening time in the life of Christendom, the Spirit of God was poured out and the world was forevermore changed.

These four weeks are designed to help your family give attention to these seasons with God at the center. Use the study the week prior to the holiday. As you continue to celebrate in your traditional fashion, set the festivities in the context of faith and pause to explore God's presence in every day.

Part 1
Inner Life

1 Acceptance:
Trust the Source

Adult Reflection

At times acceptance comes easily with great delight, as when we are offered a beautiful gift wrapped in sparkling paper and topped with a bright ribbon. We treasure the gifts that warm us in a sometimes cold and indifferent world. Some of these gifts might include friendships and family, love, community, children at play, sunsets and quiet peace within ourselves.

But what happens when our lives are touched by other rhythms, such as struggle, disappointment, loss, pain, grief and suffering? At these times we find the gift of life harder to bear and more difficult to see. Yet even in the midst of enormous tragedies God brings us new gifts. A friend unexpectedly comforts us, others draw closer to us and sometimes we find new relationships. Our rough edges are smoothed by compassion and wisdom, our judging natures are mellowed and we find we can reach out to others in their pain more readily.

The gift we receive is actually secondary. Our greatest gift is that we are called to the giver and to God. God is loving and trustworthy. We can place our trust and confidence in God's hands without fear and without regret.

Family Reflection

As you look back over this past week, you probably had a favorite day and a day that wasn't so great. Life is like that too. Some things happen in our lives that are the greatest, and some things really seem so hard—like our best friend moving away or losing a much-loved pet. Being able to accept these things and move on with our lives does not mean we will feel them any less. We will still feel very happy with the good and very sad, lonely or even angry with the not-so-good. The most important part of our lives is knowing that God loves us more than anything else in the world. God loves us in the best and the worst moments, and God will see us through both.

Day 1. God Provides for All Needs. Matthew 6:25-34.
1. What two things are we encouraged to seek?
2. What things are you most worried about today? Pray that God will give you peace, release from those worries and the security to move beyond them.

Day 2. God Loves the World. John 3:1-16.
1. How did God show the world that he loves us?
2. Have you accepted God's most precious gift? What difference has this gift made in your life?

Day 3. Under Grace. Romans 6.
1. According to Paul, what is the price of God's gift of eternal life?
2. What are some ways your life shows that you have accepted this gift?

Day 4. The Greatest Gift. 1 Corinthians 13:1-13.
1. What words describe love?
2. How do you show love to those closest to you?

Day 5. Suffering for the Gospel. 2 Timothy 1:1-12.
1. What kind of spirit does God give?
2. What things are you afraid or embarrassed to speak up about? Pray for God's courage.

Day 6. Every Perfect Gift Is from Above. James 1.

1. What does the testing of our faith produce?

2. What actions do you take to care for those less fortunate?

Special Activity: Friends

Look around your house for an object that represents a gift you have accepted from God. Put your object in a box or bag. Wrap it up if you like and bring it to the table. Listen as each member of the family shares the meaning of their gift, personally accepted from God. Open the boxes together and display the "gifts" on the table for a while as a reminder of all that God has given your family.

2 Anger:
Is It Bad to Be Mad?

Adult Reflection

In a world that tries so hard at what we deem civilized behavior, the expression of anger—in fact, even the permission to be angry—has been judged "unholy." We sometimes do not understand righteous anger because we have been taught to be loving and accepting, without rancor or judgment. But when is anger the most appropriate reaction?

What we seek is a measuring stick, a standard against which to prop our own bedraggled emotions so that we might measure their merit and appropriateness. Since we do not trust our own emotions and reactions, we look outside of ourselves for a mirror that will reflect the true picture.

Anger is part of Scripture's understanding of the character and nature of God and many of God's people. Thus we can allow Scripture to be our mirror. As we explore the triggers that moved God and others to anger, perhaps we can see a reflection of our own passion.

Family Reflection

Our feelings aren't good or bad, they are just our feelings. But it is important to know what kinds of things make us angry, so that we can be ready to handle our anger.

When does anger hurt us and the people we care about? What do we do with our angry feelings? We could stomp our feet and shout, "It's not fair!" or live alone and not speak to people, but that probably wouldn't solve anything. We could learn how to talk about our anger or draw our feelings, even to punch a pillow if we needed to! And when something really deserves our anger, like someone being mean to your friend or to animals, we could use our anger to help us change the situation.

Day 1. Moses Doubts God. Exodus 4:1-17.

God is preparing to send Moses to Pharaoh. Moses encounters God in a burning bush on the mountain of Horeb.

1. Why was God angry with Moses?

How did God respond to the concerns of Moses even though God was angry?

2. When have you felt angry with another person but were able to help them anyway?

Day 2. God's Anger Does Not Last. Psalm 30:1-12.

1. What is the difference between God's anger and God's favor?

2. Try to remember an old situation that still makes you angry. When you are angry, how long does it take for you to move past it?

Discuss ways that will help you to let go of your anger.

Day 3. Jonah Angered by God's Grace. Jonah 4:1-11.

The people of the city of Nineveh have listened to Jonah's call to turn their lives away from sin. God has decided not to punish them as he had previously promised.

1. Why was Jonah angry with God and with Nineveh?

2. Remember a time when you felt someone was unfairly angry with you. How did they express their anger?

How could they have handled their feelings better?

Day 4. Jesus and the Moneychangers. Mark 11:1-18.

1. Why was Jesus angry with the people at the entrance of the temple?

2. What kinds of things make you angry?

Day 5. Paul Calls the Ephesians to Unity. Ephesians 4:25-32.
1. What does Paul mean when he says, "Be angry but do not sin"?
2. List some positive ways we can express our anger, ways that will help us heal, move on or help others to do the same.

Day 6. Parents and Children: Mutual Respect. Ephesians 6:1-4.
1. How are parents and children advised to treat one another?
2. Discuss as a family some of the ongoing battles you fight with each other (clean room, curfew, grades and so forth) and how you could deal with these problems better.

3 Depression:
The Great Nothing

Adult Reflection

In the children's book *The Never Ending Story,* a fairy tale kingdom is being swallowed up piece by piece by a "Great Nothing." As the child reader has lost his dreams, the Great Nothing rolls across the land, destroying all in its path.

Depression is like the Great Nothing. When we find ourselves caught in its grip, a wall separates us from our own feelings. This isn't always bad; sometimes the circumstances of our lives are too painful to bear and numbing works for the good. But depression becomes destructive when we remain numb and paralyzed, unable to move forward, and when hopelessness becomes the room where we live.

Even in the wake of this Great Nothing, even in the dry wasteland of our own hopelessness, we will find the Spirit of God. God is not a passive spirit silently waiting for our returned passion but a relentless lover in pursuit.

Family Reflection

There are times when we aren't very happy. Sometimes we cry and feel very lonely. Sometimes we aren't even sure why we feel this way! When we are depressed, we feel not only sad but also like we will never be happy again. Yet even when we feel like we have no love to give, we can count on being loved by God and not having to work through our trouble alone.

Day 1. Moses Carries a Heavy Burden. Numbers 11:1-15.
1. What had happened to make Moses feel so overwhelmed?
2. What responsibilities do you have that sometimes overwhelm you? As a family, talk about how these responsibilities can be shared.

Day 2. Job's Spirits Are Broken. Job 17:1-16.
1. Many people offered Job advice. How much of this does Job think is wise?
2. Who do you count on for encouragement and advice when your spirits are down?

Day 3. Thirsting for God in Trouble. Psalm 42.
1. What question does the psalmist's enemy taunt him with?
2. Remember a time when you felt deserted by your friends and even by God. How was your relationship healed?

Day 4. Loss of a Child. 2 Samuel 12:13-18.
David has been deceitful with the soldier Uriah. He has sent him to the front lines of a battle to ensure his death so he can have Uriah's wife, Bathsheba.
1. What were David's servants afraid he would do upon hearing of his baby's death?
2. What things comforted you when someone you were close to died?

Day 5. Recalling Job's Complaints: Personal Distress. Lamentations 3:1-24.
This is an individual's reflection on the sadness of the Hebrew people, left desolate following the destruction of Jerusalem. The writer uses Job's complaints to explain the sadness of the city's population.
1. What has changed for the writer since he has forgotten what

happiness is?

How does he manage to hang on?

2. What promise do you find in these verses that might help you face each day?

Day 6. Mary and Martha Grieve. John 11:1-7, 11-44.

1. What did both Mary and Martha say to Jesus when they saw him?

2. What questions do you have for God concerning something that is making you sad? Pray for God to provide understanding and trust.

Special Activity: Feelings

Take time to think for a moment about the members of your family and the things that matter most to each of them. While you are thinking, begin using blocks, Legos, cans from your pantry or anything else you have to build a wall together down the center of your table. Now ask someone in your family either "How do you really feel about _____ ?" or "What is it like for you when _____ ?" Without offering criticism or advice, listen carefully to the response you receive. Give everyone a turn to ask and answer a question. Every time a question is answered, remove one of the blocks from your wall.

4 Fear:
It's Bigger Than Me

Adult Reflection

Following the birth of my daughter, Sarah, I remember being so immediately swept into such a passionate, intimate love for this little stranger that my own emotions shocked me. What surprised me even more, however, was my fear. This love seemed so big that I felt as though I would be consumed by it, and even more than that was the fear of ever having to live *without* her and this consuming love.

Through this experience, the Scriptures that describe those who had the "fear of the Lord" became much more understandable. One of the basics of every good relationship is a strong dose of healthy respect for the gift we are to one another. When you mix respect and honor with the overwhelming love God has for each of us, the result is so passionate, so intimate and so very demanding that we have no choice but to fear it—and to fear even more not having it.

Fear becomes negative, however, when we allow it to paralyze us and keep us from being able to grow and enjoy life. We can be sure of only one thing: whatever scene we walk into, whatever beginnings or endings we face, whatever failures, disappointments or losses await us, God's love is bigger. Nothing can separate us from the love of God.

Family Reflection

Everyone has fears. Some people are afraid to leave their closet doors open at night or dangle their foot over the side of the bed while sleeping. Some people can't set foot on an airplane. Others are afraid of getting poor grades or not being liked by a certain group. Another kind of fear is very good to have. It keeps you from touching fire or running into a busy street. This fear is based on remembering what might happen if you do those things. Whatever fears you have, God's love is bigger than anything that makes you afraid.

Day 1. Midwives Disobey the King. Exodus 1:1-22.
1. Why did the midwives Shiphrah and Puah disobey the king?
2. When have you felt pushed to act in a way you know God wouldn't like? What did you do?

Day 2. Fear: The Beginning of Wisdom. Psalm 111.
1. How can you "practice" the fear of the Lord?
2. What do you think God looks like?
   In what ways does God seem frightening to you?

Day 3. Esther Risks Her Life. Esther 5—7.
Haman has plotted to have the Jewish people executed, including Mordecai, who at one time saved the king from assassination. Going against custom and approaching the king without being summoned puts Esther's life in jeopardy; fortunately the king reacts favorably.
1. What request does Esther bring before the king?
2. Esther was afraid, yet she did what she knew she must. Is there a problem you are afraid to face? What is it?
   Pray together that God will help you overcome the fear to move forward.

Day 4. Jesus Makes a Promise. Matthew 28.
1. The resurrection and ascension leave the followers of Jesus fearful and amazed. What is the last promise Jesus leaves them with?
2. Change can be very hard and sometimes frightening, whether it's changing schools, jobs, growing up or growing old. What

changes are you facing right now? Remember, the promises of Jesus belong to you.

Day 5. Paul and Silas Are Freed from Prison. Acts 16:16-34.
1. How did the jailer's fear help him?
2. Sometimes "near misses" help us make changes that are for the better. These near misses could range from a brush with death to almost getting caught cheating. How has a close call helped to change your life in a good way?

Day 6. Our Salvation. Philippians 2:1-18.
1. How should we approach our salvation? Why?
2. The most important things are approached with respect and care. Approaching our salvation means approaching God. How do you see God at work in you?

5 Forgiveness:
You Matter More

Adult Reflection

Bitterness and resentment eat away at our abilities to be productive, loving individuals. All our energy must go toward maintaining that bitterness. This malignancy leaves little room for growth and healing, and we can become lost or stagnated.

Forgiveness doesn't necessarily mean reconciliation, it means moving past the hurt and working toward wholeness. In other cases forgiveness may mean that someone, and your relationship with him or her, means more to you than any issue or event that threatens to separate you. Often this extracts a very high price—your pride, preferences, habits, even your principles. But somewhere along the line you decide that these things are negotiable. What you find you cannot live without is the opportunity to love and be loved by the other person.

What is absolutely amazing and mind-boggling is that God embraces us with forgiveness in this very same way. God paid a price beyond comprehension in order to forgive us. God thirsts after us and our love. God is the author of this thirst and the creator of the water that quenches.

Family Reflection

We look around at our family (mother, father, sister, brother, husband, wife, child), and we know that these are the most important people in our lives. Sure, at times we feel very unhappy with them. We may even wish we could try to live without them for just a little while. But way down inside, we don't want to be without them.

When a first punch is thrown or harsh, uncaring words are hurled, a cool-down time will help with our feelings. In the long run, however, it's how much that person means to us that will help us to forgive. God loves us in the same way. Scripture tells us that sometimes God is angry with us, but God does not let anger keep us apart. He chases after us with forgiveness because he loves us so very much. Isn't that incredible?

Day 1. A Brother's Story of Forgiveness. Genesis 27:37-45; 33:1-18.

Esau has treated his birthright with little respect and sold it to his brother Jacob for a bowl of soup. Jacob has tricked Esau out of his father's blessing, which means that Esau loses his rights and properties as the firstborn.

1. How does Esau feel about Jacob in chapter 27?

How does he treat Jacob?

2. Has anyone ever treated you unfairly, or have you treated someone else unfairly?

Day 2. God Brings Good Out of Evil. Genesis 45.

Joseph's brothers were jealous of him, so they sold him into slavery in Egypt and told their father that he was dead. After many years and a severe famine, the brothers travel to Egypt to find food. There they meet Joseph, whom they do not recognize and who has become a powerful leader among the Egyptians.

1. Who does Joseph believe caused him to end up in Egypt, and why?

2. How might the story have ended had Joseph not forgiven his brothers?

Tell about a time you forgave someone for something they

did to you. How would your life be different now if you had not forgiven that person?

Day 3. Ezra Reminds the People of God's Forgiving Nature. Nehemiah 9:6-17.

The Hebrew people have returned from exile and must now begin to rebuild their religious heritage, including respect for the law, the temple and the character of God. Ezra offers a prayer that gives witness to God's faithful action throughout their history.

1. How does Ezra describe God?

2. What can we do to be "ready to forgive"?

Day 4. The Lord's Prayer. Matthew 6:5-15.

1. What does God know before we ask?

2. Accepting forgiveness is sometimes the first step in being able to experience it and offer it to others. Talk about how you have experienced forgiveness for yourself. (This could be forgiveness from God or from another person.)

Day 5. Measuring Forgiveness. Matthew 18:21-35.

The number seven held particular significance for the Jewish people. Throughout Scripture it represents the idea of fulfillment, completion or perfection.

1. Why is the king angry with his servant in this parable?

2. We ask for God's forgiveness regularly. How is this different from or the same as others asking for our forgiveness?

Day 6. Stephen Is Martyred. Acts 7:51-60.

Stephen has approached the Jewish community with witness to Christ. His words have enraged the religious leaders, who have plotted against him and falsely accused him of blasphemy. At that time stoning was a legal punishment for breaking certain religious rules.

1. What did Stephen do while he was being stoned?

2. False words and unfair actions can often hurt us. Has anyone ever deliberately lied about you? As you share this experience, pray for that person and ask God to help you begin to forgive them.

Special Activity: Breaking the Links

Think for a moment about the issues and events that threaten to separate you from the members of your family. Is there someone you are really mad at? Is there some way you were once wronged that you have never forgotten? On separate strips of paper, write it all down.

Glue the strips together to make a chain. During the next week, take the chain apart link by link, day by day. To take off some of the links you may need to talk to the person you have not forgiven. Other days you may need to destroy a link by praying. It is possible that some links in the chain will be too big for you to handle, and you will want to ask a pastor or counselor to help you with it. If you cannot destroy the entire chain in a week, make a plan that will help you to keep working on it.

6 Grief:
Too Deep for Words

Adult Reflection

When we lose someone or something that we cherish, whether through a painful event like death or divorce or through the natural course of life—growing up, growing old, growing different—there is pain and a need for healing. We feel the pain of our loss in our bodies, our spirits, our minds and our hearts. There is no place where we do not run headlong into it. Grief becomes our companion and, in some mysterious way, a friend to help us heal. Grief is a way of paying homage. If the object of our grief were not so deeply cherished, it most certainly would not be so missed.

The grief of God is an awesome subject to contemplate. That this Creator of the universe, this maker, this source of being should grieve for a relationship with us is almost too incredible to imagine.

Family Reflection

It is very important to us to be able to touch and hold the people, animals and things that we love. When we can't do this because they are lost or have died, we feel very sad, afraid or even angry. At times we feel like a great big balloon with all the air let out. But we feel all these things for a really great reason—because we had so much love. Time helps us not to hurt so much when we think about who or what we've lost. After a while, we aren't so afraid to think about them, and then our memories help make us happy.

God loves us so very much and felt grief when sin made us lost. Jesus came because God couldn't stand to lose us. He came to help us understand how much we are loved.

Day 1. Hannah Longs for a Child. 1 Samuel 1:1-27.
1. As Hannah shows her sadness, what does Elkanah think of
her behavior?
2. Describe the saddest time that you can remember. What were
some of the ways you showed your sadness?

Day 2. David Mourns for Saul and Jonathan. 2 Samuel 1:1-27.
1. What did David do to make sure the memory of Saul and
Jonathan would be kept alive?
2. Share a few memories about someone who has died.

Day 3. Jesus Laments over Jerusalem. Matthew 23:37-39.
1. What grieved Jesus about Jerusalem?
2. How would you try to comfort and protect someone you
loved?

Day 4. Mary and Martha Grieve for Lazarus. John 11:1-46.
1. How did Martha greet Jesus when he finally arrived?
2. Who brings you the most comfort when you are sad? Explain
how he or she makes you feel better.

Day 5. Dorcas Is Raised from the Dead. Acts 9:32-43.
1. Describe the kind of person Dorcas was.
2. What kinds of things would you want others to remember
about you?

Day 6. A New Heaven. Revelation 21:1-6.
1. What are the promises given in these verses?
2. If you were creating a brand new world, what things would
you make different?

7 Guilt:
Twisting on the Hook

Adult Reflection

Guilt is painful, no doubt about it. First, we face the painful reality of consequences that must follow some action we have taken. That we have chosen this particular road makes us feel all the more wretched.

Even if no one but God knows our guilt, the pain of living within the skin of someone we don't particularly respect may paralyze us. Sometimes living with the secret knowledge that we do not deserve the trust of the people around us makes us push away the very thing we need the most—their love.

God has the ability and the right to nail us for our deceptive and hurtful actions. And yet in an unfathomable act of sheer love, God took those nails into his own body.

We must still deal with our own behaviors and choices but, because of the choices God has made, we can wake up every morning with hope for a new day.

Family Reflection

We can feel guilt in two ways, and neither one is very pleasant. The first is when we are caught doing something we have been told not to do. The other is when we don't get caught, and we have that awful feeling inside. We might feel like we don't deserve a warm hug or trusting smile, so we start acting up— trying to make sure no one hugs us or smiles at us. What an awful mess!

The good news is that our guilt can help us stop doing things that might hurt us or others. We can try not to make the same mistakes over again. The really good news is that God loves us so much that our guilt is taken away, and we are given the chance to start fresh—over and over again!

Day 1. Adam and Eve Disobey God. Genesis 3:1-10.
1. Why were Adam and Eve hiding from God?
2. Have you ever tried to keep secret something you had done wrong? How did you feel?

Day 2. Israel Sends Home Foreign Wives and Children. Ezra 9:1—10:5.
The Hebrew people have returned from exile to the Promised Land, bringing with them many foreign wives and children, even though the Lord had told them not to marry people who worshiped other gods.
1. How did the people respond to Ezra's plea to make right their guilt?
2. The Hebrew men who had married foreign wives had sinned. They were given a chance to make things right. How would you go about making things right for something you had done wrong?

Day 3. The Guilt of Judas. Matthew 27:1-8.
1. Rather than live with the guilt of what he had done, Judas made another choice. What was his choice?
2. Even with the worst sin, God can forgive us and help us feel clean again. Pray for one another, that each of you might feel the forgiveness of God and the encouragement to start over.

Day 4. Peter Denies Christ. Mark 14:66-72.
Jesus has been arrested and taken to face his accusers. Peter has followed at a distance and now waits for him in the lower courtyard.

1. Why did Peter feel bad about the way he acted?

2. Try to think of an experience when you should have stood up for a friend or a family member but didn't. Perhaps you even joined in the teasing or gossip. How did this make a difference in your relationship with that person?

Day 5. The Adulterous Woman. John 8:1-11.

1. Who did Jesus tell to throw the first stone?

2. Try to think of someone who is guilty of wrongdoing against you. How does this particular Scripture apply to you?

Day 6. Ananias and Sapphira Caught in a Lie. Acts 4:31—5:12.

1. What was the lie that Ananias and Sapphira told?

2. What happened to these two people seems harsh. But think of a time that people were allowed to get away with lies. What was the result?

Special Activity: Confession

Give each person one nail and a piece of paper. On your paper write your name and something you have felt guilty over. If you have never confessed your sin before, take a moment to do that and to forgive others as necessary. Now take two boards and nail them together in the shape of a cross. Let every member of your family nail his or her paper to the boards. Thank God for nailing your guilt and sin to the cross through his Son, Jesus. Rejoice because you are forgiven, and God loves you very much.

8 Hope:
I Wish I May, I Wish I Might

Adult Reflection

Hoping and wishing have much in common. Each one represents a confidence that there is some chance, however slim, that what we want can come true. They part company, however, when they are weighed within the drama of human need. We might very well move comfortably through our lives without expecting our wishes to come exactly true. But it is frightening to meet a person without hope. Before Jesus, the world was without hope. Because of him we can now have full confidence that God's promises can be ours.

Family Reflection

Wishes and hopes are alike in some ways, but there is also a big difference. For example, you are waiting to find out your grade on a big test. If you had spent your study time watching TV or playing with friends, you may *wish* that somehow you stumbled on the right answers and won't have to spend a weekend earning extra credit. But if you actually did study and prepare as best you could, you have every right to *hope* for a good grade. Because of Jesus, we can have hope for the future.

Day 1. Abram Is Promised a Son. Genesis 15:1-21.

1. What promise does God make to Abram?

2. Tell about something you are hoping for.

Day 2. David Challenges Goliath. 1 Samuel 17:31-52.

1. How does David think he can beat Goliath?

2. What is the greatest challenge you are facing today? Tell each other about it, and talk about ways to meet these challenges.

Day 3. New Heavens and New Earth. Isaiah 65:17-25.

1. What promises does God make in these verses?

2. What changes described in these verses do you think the world needs most right now?

Day 4. A Woman's Bleeding Is Stopped. Mark 5:21-34.

1. How had the woman tried to help herself before she went to Jesus?

2. Have you ever tried lots of solutions to a problem before you remembered to ask for God's help? Talk about what happened.

Day 5. Jesus' Birth Is Foretold. Luke 1:26-45.

1. How does the angel assure Mary that all that has been said will come true?

2. God can use each of us in very special ways. How might God use you to bring hope to others?

Day 6. The Resurrection of Jesus. John 20:1-31.

1. What does the writer say is the specific reason for recording this account of Jesus' resurrection?

2. Describe how your life has changed because of the resurrection of Christ.

9 Joy:
A *Tap* on the *Shoulder*

Adult Reflection

It's hard to talk about joy: the very essence of the experience defies definition. It is much easier to talk about joy's occasions—the moments when, without rhyme or reason, we find ourselves tapped on the shoulder and embraced by completeness and *rightness*.

Such an experience came to me shortly after I was married. The moment was really quite ordinary. My husband, Phil, and I were walking from our apartment to our friends' home. Phil was carrying a watermelon, and I had all our games—Scrabble, Monopoly, playing cards. We weren't even talking, just walking together. As we walked, I looked around: the trees seemed wonderfully green, the sky so intensely blue. When I looked at Phil, an overwhelming sense of completeness took my breath from me. For just a brief moment I knew that I was exactly where I should be, with exactly whom I must be with.

That was sixteen years ago. Other moments of sheer serendipitous pleasure have come—the births of my children, for example. Still, the memory of that moment so many years ago stands out in my mind and brings me lasting delight.

Family Reflection

Have you ever had just one more piece to fit to make a puzzle complete? When you found it, you may have shouted out loud, or maybe you just sat back and smiled. Have you ever, for no good reason whatsoever, felt laughter bubble up and come bursting out? Or have you ever been so glad to just be who you are? That's joy! God wants us to have so much joy that we might even begin to understand how he feels about us. Joy is God's special gift for us.

Day 1. A Psalm of Thanks. Psalm 100.

1. What main reason does the psalmist give for a spirit of gladness?

2. What do you know about God that brings you the most joy?

Day 2. The Birth of Christ. Luke 2:1-20.

1. What good news did the angel bring?

2. What was the best news you have ever received?

Day 3. The Lost Sheep. Luke 15:1-7.

1. What will bring the most rejoicing in heaven?

2. Have you ever lost something that was very precious to you? What was it? How did you feel when you either found it or knew you'd lost it for good?

Day 4. The Lame Beggar Walks. Acts 3:1-10.

1. What did the lame man expect to get from Peter and John?

2. Sometimes what we ask God for is much less than what he has planned for us. Talk about what you have been asking from God. Pray for wisdom and openness to God's leading.

Day 5. Complete Joy. Philippians 2:1-11.

1. How does Paul say his joy could be made complete?

2. In what ways do you or don't you put what other people want before what you want?

Day 6. Joy Beyond Words. 1 Peter 1:3-9.

1. What does the writer say is the cause of "an indescribable and glorious joy" (v. 8)?

2. Have you ever been so full of joy that you couldn't even speak? Tell about your experience.

Special Activity: Garden of Joy

I have found joy blooming in my heart like a plant. God was the gardener that grew it there. Suffering and sorrow were the tools used to break up my heart's hard soil. My own tears watered the fragile plant while it grew. There were weeds to pull, and that hurt. And then, one day, all of a sudden, joy was there, and it felt wonderful.

Plant a garden of joy with your family today. In a flower box prepare the soil and carefully plant your seeds. Delight in watering and caring for your little garden, and celebrate as the first flowers appear. As you work, talk together about the things that bring you joy and the areas where God is still working on you.

10 Loneliness:
In the Desert

Adult Reflection

Growing up in the desert taught me a great lesson about loneliness. You could stand at the foot of a dune and hear no sounds. Scanning the horizon, you might detect no signs of movement or life as far as the eye could see. Yet it was not in the desert that my deepest experiences of loneliness came. The greatest loneliness came when I felt disconnected, cut off emotionally, from the people around me.

Why are we so afraid to be lonely? Perhaps the fear comes because we measure our worth by our reflection in other people's eyes. Or maybe we can't stand the thoughts that come crashing in when our moments are not filled with "doing." Loneliness is not actually a place but a state of the heart. If you understand the desert, you know that it is actually not empty but teeming with life, movement and growth. We can also be sure that God will meet us in the desert of our souls, and in that meeting we can find life, movement and growth.

Family Reflection

Have you ever been in a crowd at a park or a birthday party and yet felt like you were the only person there? You were feeling so alone! Yet when a friend came over and invited you to play, all of a sudden everything seemed different. Being alone isn't necessarily bad. It gives you a chance to dream and think and just to be. Being lonely sometimes helps us to appreciate our friends and learn how to be a really good friend even more. But even in our most alone and lonely moments, it is important to remember that God is always with us.

Day 1. Elijah at Mount Horeb. 1 Kings 19.
Elijah, a prophet of God, is being hunted in order to be put to death by the wicked Queen Jezebel.
1. In what way did the Lord finally reveal himself to Elijah?
2. Tell about some unexpected ways you have met God.

Day 2. My Soul Waits in Silence. Psalm 62:1-8.
1. What does David encourage his people to do?
2. Silence can be a hard discipline to practice, but in that silence can come many wonderful things. Read verse 1 again and sit silently for at least twenty seconds. Then read verse 8.

Day 3. Jesus in the Wilderness. Matthew 4:1-11.
1. How did Jesus respond to the temptations of the devil?
2. Being alone sometimes forces us to be sad or worry. What thoughts are troubling to you?

Day 4. Jesus at Gethsemane. Matthew 26:26-46.
1. What did Jesus ask his disciples to do while he prayed?
2. Who are the people that you count on the most? Why?

Day 5. The Crucifixion of Jesus. Luke 23:32-49.
1. Where were the friends and followers of Jesus when he was being crucified?
2. Discuss how you might be able to help others when they face hard times—a new person at school, someone who is being bullied or a friend moving away, for example.

Day 6. Paul in Prison. 2 Timothy 4:9-22.
1. Who took Paul's side at his first defense?
2. There are many people in our world who need us to stand up for them. How can you help someone who needs defending?

11 Love:
The Heart of the Answer

Adult Reflection

Recently in a Communion class that included a Passover Seder, a seven-year-old boy asked me, "Why did Jesus *have* to die?"

Our faith is full of such questions. Why did God create human beings? Why did God destroy the world with a flood? Why did God send so many to try to bring us back to him? Why did God come as a baby in the middle of the night? Why did God hang on a cross and die? Why did God change all the rules and live again?

I would not presume to try to explain God's purposes. What I do know is that the heart of the answer to all those questions is love. Not love simply as an emotion but as an act of will. It is God's will to love us at any cost. It is God's will that nothing should separate us from his love. It is also God's will that we should love one another with the same depth and passion with which we are loved.

Family Reflection

It's hard to explain love, and maybe it's not meant to be explained. The Bible has some pretty good descriptions of what love is, so you'll be sure to recognize it when you see it. Most of all, though, remember that God loves you more than he loved his own life! God doesn't want anything to come between you and him. And also remember that love gets better and better the more you give it away. Jesus taught us that.

Day 1. The Friendship of David and Jonathan. 1 Samuel 20.
1. How did Jonathan help save David's life?
2. Who is your best friend?
   What things do you like most about him or her?

Day 2. The First and Second Greatest Commandments. Matthew 22:34-40.
The Pharisees and Sadducees were prominent religious leaders. They did not like the popularity Jesus received and so tried to discredit him at every opportunity. They did not generally believe that Jesus was the Christ.
1. What depended on these two commandments?
2. Who do you think your *neighbor* is?
   How can you show your neighbor love?

Day 3. God So Loved the World. John 3:16-17.
1. How did God show that he loved the world?
2. In what ways does God continue to show you how much he loves you?

Day 4. No Greater Love. John 15:7-17.
1. How does Jesus describe the greatest love?
2. Describe the most difficult thing you have ever had to do because you loved someone. (This includes things like forgiveness, second chances, saying goodby, giving away something precious, and letting another person have a turn or a chance.)

Day 5. What Shall Separate Us? Romans 8:31-39.
1. What does Paul say separates us from the love of God?
2. What kinds of things do you feel keep you from enjoying the love of God?

Day 6. The Way of Love. 1 Corinthians 13:1-13.
1. What things will pass away, and what things will never end?
2. Read verse 4 once again. Talk about this description, and think of times when someone in your family was "patient" and "kind" rather than envious or boastful.

Special Activity: Love Bunch
You will need a bunch of bananas, marking pens and a paper heart. As a family, think of someone to whom you would like to give a gift of love. (Your pastor or Sunday-school teacher might be the perfect choice.) On the heart write the words "God Loves You a Whole Bunch and So Do We!" Now have fun decorating the bananas with the markers. You may want to choose favorite Scripture verses from this week's study to write on a banana, or draw a picture or two. Deliver your gift together.

12 Shame:
Rotten to the Core

Adult Reflection

Parenting books teach parents to distinguish what their child has done from who their child is. Admonishments like "Be a good boy and eat your soup" or "What a bad little girl for not brushing your teeth!" are recognized as inappropriate, even cruel. The difference between guilt and shame is that guilt is what we feel when something we have done is wrong or bad, while shame is what we feel because we believe *who we are* is bad. If we are trapped into believing that what we do will redeem us but who we are is just plain bad, then we are in an endless cycle of shame. It won't matter how hard we work or what we achieve, because nothing will ever be enough. God, however, has always looked at us through a Maker's eyes and has placed a high value on who we are.

Family Reflection

If you are the new kid at school, the first day is always the worst. No matter what "with-it" clothes, backpack or shoes you have on, you feel like the biggest geek that ever lived. Luckily, soon you make new friends. But don't be too quick to forget that awful feeling, because next time you meet the "new kid" at school you will know just how he or she feels!

We are made in God's own image. What we do or don't do doesn't make us any less special. How we act can help us or hurt us, though, in being able to enjoy the wonderful life that God has given us.

Day 1. Adam and Eve Disobey God. Genesis 3:1-10.
1. What made Adam and Eve feel ashamed?
2. Share an experience where you have kept something hidden or secret that made you feel very bad.

Day 2. Joab Reproves David's Lament. 2 Samuel 19:1-8.
Absalom, David's son, and his army had chased David from Jerusalem. While in battle against David's army, Absalom is killed.
1. Why does Joab reprimand David for grieving for his son?
2. Think about some of the problems you are facing right now. How do you think your problems are affecting other people?

Day 3. Daniel Prays for His People. Daniel 9:1-10.
1. What does David confess to the Lord about his people?
2. What do you think about your country and its problems?

Day 4. The Woman Weeps at the Feet of Jesus. Luke 7:37-50.
1. Why did the woman cry at Jesus' feet?
2. How do you let go of the things that make you sad or ashamed?

Day 5. Jesus Heals on the Sabbath. Luke 13:10-17.
1. Why did those who spoke against Jesus feel humiliated?
2. When have you felt humiliated in front of others? Talk about how you felt and how you feel about it now.

Day 6. Be Imitators of God. Ephesians 5:1-12.
1. This passage tells us many things that we are not to do, but what does it say also brings shame to us?
2. Filling our minds with things that bring us shame can be very harmful. Talk about how you choose the music you listen to, and the television shows and movies your family watches.

13 Trust:
Beyond Belief!

Adult Reflection

A man falls over the side of a cliff and hangs on to a scraggly bit of brush. The jagged rocks just seem to be waiting for him to fall. Suddenly the Lord appears, and the man lets out a relieved "At last!" He waits to be scooped up from his perilous predicament. He fully believes the Lord will save him. Unexpectedly, he hears the voice of the Lord saying, "First you'll need to let go; then I will catch you."

We can have all the belief in the world, but until that belief is backed up with trust we cannot experience the fullness of God's saving, merciful, incredibly loving nature. Nor can we hope to experience life on solid ground. Some of us just keep hanging on to our bit of shrub for dear life—only life without God is anything but.

In letting go of our tenuous security we also must let go of our persistent need to understand and control the situation. A few synonyms for *trust* are *faith, confidence* and *dependence.* All of these suggest a full assurance that someone or something will not fail us.

As we learn to "let go," we can count on God not only to catch us but also to strengthen us for the next adventure. Somewhere along the way we will run into another stranded victim clinging to a cliff. And if we have proved ourselves trustworthy, when we dare them to let go and promise to be there for the catch, we too will experience the miracle of trust.

Family Reflection

In Walt Disney's version of *The Jungle Book,* Mowgli is almost hypnotized by a very large snake. The snake looks in his eyes and sings, "Trusssst in me, trusssst in me." We know that Mowgli would be in a lot of trouble if he trusted the snake. Mowgli had to learn who he could and could not trust, and so do we.

There really are a lot of kind people in the world, and that's pretty good news. But the best news of all is that there is someone we can count on all of the time, someone we can trust with all of our heart and soul. And that is God. God always keeps his promises and loves us more than his own life.

Day 1. Abraham Is Called to Offer Isaac. Genesis 22:1-19.
1. What did Abraham name the place where he was to sacrifice his son?

What did this name mean?
2. Sometimes it seems that God calls us to do some very hard things. Talk about some of those difficult decisions.

Day 2. Samson Places His Trust in Delilah. Judges 16:4-31.
Samson had been chosen at birth by God to be his great warrior. He was also set apart as a Nazirite. A Nazirite took special vows such as never cutting his hair, braiding it in seven locks, and never drinking wine or even eating grapes.
1. How many times did Samson allow himself to be deceived by Delilah?
2. Has someone you thought you could trust ever let you down? How did that feel?

Day 3. The Shepherd Psalm. Psalm 23.
1. What will follow the writer of this psalm all the days of his life? Why?
2. David himself had been a shepherd, so he knew the trust that goes along with that responsibility. Try changing this psalm by comparing God to someone you have learned to trust.

Day 4. Free from Worry. Matthew 6:25-34.
1. What are we urged to seek?
2. What things are you worried about today? How can your family help one another with these things? Pray together that you can find peace through trust in God's care.

Day 5. Four Thousand Fed. Mark 8:1-13.
1. The people trusted Jesus to provide for them and he did. What did the Pharisees want Jesus to give them?

How did Jesus respond?
2. Even after all that God has done for us, sometimes we test the Lord. Have you ever prayed, "If you love me you will . . ." or "I promise I'll do anything if you will only . . ."? When have you done this?

Day 6. The First Disciples. Luke 5:1-11.
1. What arrangements did the disciples make to leave their homes to follow Jesus?
2. What changes are you willing to make to follow Jesus?

Special Activity: Trust Walk
Set up an obstacle course. Then pair up and pass out blindfolds. Take turns leading each other through the obstacle course. Talk about the barriers to trust that you experience.

For example, my two-year-old, Benjy, is not a reliable guide. I never know where I'm going to end up or what I'll bump into when he leads me. That, of course, is different from the feeling that someone in my family might think it was funny to make me bump into things. The person who I know I can count on to lead me safely through the course will certainly be my favorite guide. And even this person is not as trustworthy as God!

Part 2
Family Life

14 Death:
Making All Things New

Adult Reflection

Throughout Jesus' ministry we find him knocking at doors, chipping away at walls and sometimes uprooting traditions that had stood for thousands of years. Jesus challenges the lines between servant and leader, action and intent, sick and well, chosen and unchosen, even death and life. In his resurrection miracles Jesus was not just saving one life. He was reframing the world's understanding of death. By redefining our reality, he was preparing us for the gift of a new hope. Although Jesus appeared to be changing everything, he was actually reintroducing the world to the heart of God.

Family Reflection

God never, never breaks any kind of promises or agreements. One of his rules was that if we acted in ways that would keep us and others away from his love, if we sinned, then when our life was over it was really over! But because God loves us so much that he could not bear to be separated from us, God needed to think of a way to give us another chance without breaking his own rules. So he sent his only Son, Jesus, to die for us. When Jesus rose from the dead, that made it possible for every single one of us to know, without any doubt, that death is not the end, but a change. We will leave this life, and that might seem sad or scary, but it helps to know that there is a place to be with God, and in that place life has no end.

Day 1. Our Days Are like the Grass. Psalm 103:6-22.
1. Our days are numbered, but what is everlasting to everlasting?
2. What things in your life seem most important right now?

Do you think those things will still be important five, ten and twenty years from now? Why?

Day 2. God of the Living. Mark 12:18-27.
1. How did the Sadducees try to trap Jesus?
2. Describe what you think happens when you die. Be honest and explore your thoughts openly.

Day 3. Death Through Sin. Romans 5:6-21.
1. Why did death enter the world?
2. What do you find hard to understand about death?

Day 4. Nothing in All Creation. Romans 8:31-39.
1. What things does Paul say *cannot* separate us from the love of God?
2. Think of someone who is going through a hard time. Would something in this passage help that person find hope? Take a moment to pray either silently or aloud for this individual.

Day 5. We Shall All Be Changed! 1 Corinthians 15:51-58.
1. What is the sting of death?
2. If you could change anything about your life right now, what would it be?

Day 6. Paul Prepares to Die. 2 Timothy 4:1-8.
1. Who will be awarded the crown of righteousness?
2. If you learned you were going to die tomorrow, what things in your life would make you the most proud?

15 Decisions:
The Crossroads

Adult Reflection

Imagine you come to a crossroads—a decision you are faced with right now. Does your crossroads look like a fork in a country road, or does it look like a big-city interchange? Some decisions are a choice between a right and a wrong: a fork. Other decisions range from worst to best: an interchange.

Some people believe that if things go well after their decision, they have been blessed for their wisdom. Jesus might be offended by this attitude, given where his Gethsemane decision took him. Others believe just the opposite: If your decision leads to suffering and pain, it is most certainly in keeping with the will of God!

For Christians, making good decisions is connected to understanding and committing ourselves to the will of God. And what is the will of God? The answer to that can be found in the Gospel of Mark, quoting Deuteronomy 6:4-8.

> Hear, O Israel: The Lord our God, the Lord is one; you shall love the Lord your God with all your heart, and with all your soul, and with all your mind, and with all your strength. . . . You shall love your neighbor as yourself. (Mark 12:29-31)

So you stand at the crossroads and make your choice, but just before you step onto the path a strong, weather-worn hand slips into yours and holds on tight. You turn to see Jesus. He whispers, "Are you ready?" You nod your head, and he says, "Then let's go."

Family Reflection

Some decisions are fun to make: "What kind of ice cream do I want at my party?" "Should I ride my bike or rollerblade to my friend's house?" Other decisions are not so fun: "Should I tell my teacher I saw Jim cheating?" "Should I watch a TV program my parents told me not to?" "Should I live with my mom or with my dad?"

It can be pretty tough trying to make the best possible choices. The Bible tells us that the most important thing for us to remember and to do is "love the Lord your God with all your heart, and with all your soul, and with all your strength, and with all your mind" and to "love your neighbor as yourself."

So when tough decisions roll around try asking yourself a couple of questions: "Which choice would help me love God more?" "Which choice might hurt another person?" And, remember, you can count on Jesus to love you all the way through your choices.

Day 1. Israel Decides to Have a King. 1 Samuel 8:1-22; 9:15-17.
1. What did God do after the people chose to ignore his advice?
2. Tell about a bad decision you have made. As you look back, do you see that any good things have come out of this unwise decision? What good things do you see?

Day 2. David Prays for Wisdom in His Decisions. Psalm 143.
1. What does David want the Lord to teach him?
2. If the enemies in this psalm were the things or people who are stopping you from making important decisions, who or what would they be?

Day 3. Meshach, Shadrach and Abednego Decide for God. Daniel 3:8-18.
1. What was the most important decision facing Meshach, Shadrach and Abednego?

2. The decision of these young men did not depend on what God would do for them as a result. What kinds of bargains have you made with God in the past?

Day 4. The Decision of the Rich Young Ruler. Mark 10:17-22.
Jesus continues teaching in the region of Judea, attracting crowds along the way.
1. What did the rich young man decide to do after speaking with Jesus?
2. What things would be hard to give up if Jesus asked you to? Remember, it may not be wrong to own things, but it is always wrong to love our possessions more than we love God.

Day 5. A Decision of Betrayal. Matthew 26:6-16, 20-25, 47-50; 27:1-5.
1. Judas made several decisions on his way to betray Jesus. What was his first decision? What was his last?
2. What decisions have you made that you still regret? Pray together that God will heal you from guilt, blame and remorse. Pray also that God can work good through even your worst decisions.

Day 6. Peter and John's Decision to Preach. Acts 4:1-23.
Peter and John have healed a lame beggar and are preaching Christ with great confidence.
1. What decision did Peter and John face?
2. What is the most important decision you are facing today? Who can help you talk this over and think about the consequences?

Special Activity: Decision Game
Give each person five slips of paper. On each piece of paper

write down one decision that you face in the next week. When everyone is finished, mix the slips of paper together. These are your "decision cards."

On a floor, counter or table, use a long piece of string to make a maze like the one in the diagram. Tape the string down so that it will maintain its shape. Each person will need to select a small household object to be their playing piece in the maze.

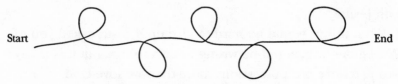

As the game begins, player 1 goes to the first intersection. A decision card is then read out loud. The player must share one loving way to respond to the situation on the card. After the player has responded, the family votes on whether the decision was truly loving. If the decision was loving, the player proceeds to the next intersection on his next turn. If the decision was not loving, the player must go through the feedback loop and repeat the same intersection by drawing another decision card on the next turn. Continue playing until all of the decision cards have been read and someone has finished the maze.

16 Discipline: *Sink or Swim*

Adult Reflection

Many people think of *discipline* as synonymous with *punishment*. But punishment aims for a behavior change, while discipline is designed to facilitate a heart change. We know that a heart change will ultimately lead to a behavior change, but changed behavior may not lead to a changed heart. We can forbid young Anthony to pour milk (punishment), or we can buy smaller cartons, mark the glass with a line for full and show him where we keep the paper towels and cleanser (discipline).

In *Making All Things New,* Henri Nowen says that "discipline is the other side of discipleship. The practice of spiritual discipline makes us more sensitive to the small, gentle voice of God." Our lives have become so hectic and overfilled that we are unfulfilled. We need discipline because we need to learn to listen to God

Family Reflection

How long can you hold your breath? Can you not speak a single word for five whole minutes? Do you do *all* of your homework right after school? Can you jump rope or ride a bike? Can you snap your fingers, whistle or blow bubbles with your chewing gum? Learning all of these skills requires discipline. It takes a lot of practice, probably some frustration and maybe even a skinned knee or two, to get the job done.

Discipline is meant to prepare you to do all the wonderful things you have always wanted to do—and to feel pretty good about yourself while you're doing them. Discipline is also meant to prepare you to be the kind of person God always intended you to be. Sometimes the road of discipline is rough, but it's a road we can count on to get us where we need to go.

Day 1. God Equips Moses. Exodus 3:9-12; 4:1-5, 10-17.

God has appeared to Moses in the burning bush on Mount Horeb, and he is now ready to call him to go to Egypt to free the Israelites from their slavery.

1. How did God respond to Moses every time he voiced his fears and uncertainty?

2. Sometimes we feel like the jobs we are given are too big. What jobs do you feel are too big for you? Discuss how you can help each other to learn to get these jobs done.

Day 2. A Wise Child. Proverbs 13:1-4.

Proverbs contains several collections of sayings. The purpose of the book is to give insights to help a youth to cope with life.

1. Whose appetite is satisfied in these verses?

What does this idea mean to you?

2. What things are done for you that you wish you knew how to do for yourself?

How could you go about learning how to do them?

Day 3. Our Words Count. Proverbs 15:1-5.

1. How are a gentle tongue and a perverse tongue different?

2. Have you ever lost your temper and said things you did not mean? What happened between you and the other person?

How could it have been handled differently?

Day 4. Jesus Is Tempted. Luke 4:1-13.

1. How did Jesus respond every single time he was tempted?

2. Jesus had prepared himself for what he encountered in the world. How do you prepare yourself?

Day 5. The Disciples Argue. Mark 9:33-37.
Jesus has just healed a boy who was unable to hear or speak. He and the disciples are now traveling to Capernaum.
1. What were the disciples arguing about?
2. Jesus deals with the issue of the argument rather than the disciples' behavior. Talk about the most recent argument you have had. What do you feel was given the most attention, the behavior or the issue?

Day 6. Discipline for Christian Ministry. 1 Timothy 4:1-16.
1. What things must we insist on and teach?
2. How does your family equip themselves to live a life close to God?

What are some other ways you might explore together?

Special Activity: Journaling
One of the most helpful disciplines I have developed is journaling. I begin each page with "Dear God." Sometimes I will draw a picture of a favorite Scripture passage. Some days I am writing through tears as I put into words my secret longings and deepest fears. My journal is a written record of my prayers and of my wrestling matches with God.

This week, give each person some paper for journaling. Every day write or draw a picture about your life. Communicate from your heart with your heavenly Father in whatever format feels most comfortable to you. At the end of the week, discuss the experience of keeping a journal. Provide an opportunity for anyone to share journal entries if desired.

17 Divorce:
Torn Apart

Adult Reflection

A synonym for *divorce* is *severance,* as in amputation. The comparison is certainly not far-fetched. There is always pain, pain and more pain involved when a family (and I use this term broadly) breaks apart.

Whether it's breakup of a marriage, parents and children, a church, a community or a country, the dynamics are almost identical: a relationship is built and invested in, trust and promise are exchanged, and somewhere along the line betrayal or disappointment, silence, misunderstandings, compromises and crashed dreams shake the foundation and the walls begin to tumble.

Jesus speaks quite strongly about divorce. He should know. After all, he came to reconcile the two parties involved in the greatest divorce of all. Jesus knew the terrible cost of divorce. When humankind decided to make its exit from the household of God by sinning, it was as though a part of God had been sliced away and the open wound could be seen in the hands and feet of Christ.

We aren't called to judge the lives of others, but as Christians we *are* called to love others with the same grace and compassion that have been extended to us. We can't answer every question of those who are hurting, but we can make sure that the healing presence of the Lord is felt in our words and actions.

Family Reflection

Nobody ever plans to have their marriage end in divorce. In fact, it's the last thing anyone expects to happen to them. It can be very scary and confusing when parents decide they can't stay married any longer. Sometimes kids think it's their fault because they were too loud or messy, or because they kept forgetting to take out the garbage. But this just isn't true. Parents decide to divorce each other, and that's very sad, but it's not because of their kids—no way!

God knows exactly what it feels like to go through a divorce. When God created people, he meant for us to live together and love each other and be happy always, but it just didn't turn out that way. But God never gives up on us. He even sent his own Son, Jesus, to bring us back together.

Day 1. Adam and Eve Betray God's Trust. Genesis 3:8-24.
1. Why did God make the man and woman leave the Garden and their way of life?
2. What are three of the most important rules in your home? What would happen if you broke those rules?

Day 2. Disobedience of Queen Vashti. Esther 1:10-22.
1. What was the king concerned that others would begin thinking after they had heard about the queen's refusal to come?
2. In this passage we are given only one side to the story. Talk about a time when there was a misunderstanding in your family. Have each member share what they remember as the problem and how it was solved.

Day 3. Be Faithful. Malachi 2:10-16.
1. What two things does the Lord say that he hates?
2. God wants us to be faithful in all that we do. Describe your best friend and how you show your loyalty to your friend.

Day 4. Teaching About Divorce. Mark 10:1-9.
1. How does Jesus explain that Moses would allow divorce?

2. Who do you feel closer to than anyone else? What kinds of things make you feel close?

___

Day 5. A Woman Caught in Adultery. John 8:1-11.
Adultery and immorality were the only exceptions cited by Jesus to the law against divorce. This makes Jesus' actions all the more extraordinary. See Matthew 19:9.
1. What would have happened to this woman if Jesus had not been there?
2. We have all done things we are ashamed of. Jesus loves us and is there for us no matter what. Pray together that God can help us to move ahead without shame and guilt. Pray also that God can help you not to do things that cause you shame.

___

Day 6. The Sanctity of Marriage. 1 Corinthians 7:10-17.
1. How does Paul encourage the Corinthians to live?
2. We are encouraged to lead the lives that God has assigned to us. Share your thoughts about what kind of life you have been assigned and how you will go about living it.

18 Family:
The Glorious Journey

Adult Reflection

We are barraged with news about the disintegration of the "family" and how its demise is affecting the culture. It is true that our families are facing many tough issues, but families have struggled with tough issues since time and sin began. What is amazing, even miraculous, is that even in the midst of our experiences with divorce, violence, poverty, disease and absentee parents, the need for family and the effort to create that connection remains strong.

The face of the family may seem different these days. We have grandparents raising grandchildren as their own, single parents, blended families, stepfamilies. But whatever the shape, we can rejoice that God has in some incredible, mysterious act of grace bound us together to share the glorious journey we call *family*.

Family Reflection

Have you ever heard someone say, "He's just like one of the family"? You may have even said this yourself about someone you really care about. When we talk about our family, we are usually talking about people we love and trust. But it's really more than that. When someone is part of our family, we feel like we can count on them. We feel comfortable being with them. We feel like we can watch Saturday morning cartoons in our pajamas with them and not even be embarrassed!

In your family you may have parents, grandparents, sisters, brothers, aunts, uncles and cousins. At your dinner table you may have enough people for a baseball team. Or your family might be your mom or dad and you—just enough people to fly a beautiful kite on a windy day. God calls us his children, and that makes us a family. It's really nice to know that we have so many people to love and who love us.

Day 1. Ruth and Naomi. Ruth 1:1-22.
1. Why did Naomi want to send her daughters-in-law back to their homes?
2. What kind of things are happening in your life that make you really count on your family sticking together? Share ways that you can better support one another through these times.

Day 2. David's Last Words to His Son Solomon. 1 Kings 2:1-4.
1. How does David advise Solomon to succeed?
2. After spending a few moments in thought, go around the family circle and say in one or two sentences what you think is the secret of success.

Day 3. Mary and Martha. Luke 10:38-42.
Jesus has just appointed the seventy to go out as his disciples, and they have returned rejoicing with their success in sharing the good news.
1. Why was Martha upset with Mary?
2. When was the last time you were upset with your sister or brother? What happened and how you were able to get over it? If you are not reconciled with your brother or sister, stop now and as a family pray for healing and forgiveness.

Day 4. Jesus Cares for His Mother. John 19:16-30.
1. What kind of arrangements did Jesus make to have his mother cared for?
2. Many of us spend most of our time with people who are not

the most significant people in our lives. How does your family make sure that you have time to be together in work and play?

Think of some new ways you can make time for one another.

Day 5. The Family Name. Ephesians 3:14-21.
1. Paul writes that all families, in heaven and on earth, are bound together. According to Paul, what connects all of us?
2. What are some things that you think might be the same in any family no matter where you searched, even if you went to China, Germany or the North Pole?

Day 6. Family Relationships. Ephesians 6:1-4.
1. What makes this commandment different from the others?
2. Perhaps you have allowed certain things to be sore points over and over again in your family—clean room, curfew, homework, finances. Talk together about ways each of you can help change the way you deal with the sore points.

Special Activity: Being Together
At least three evenings a week when 7:30 rolls around, I'm in the kitchen making popcorn and pouring glasses of cold apple cider. My four children come running and gather around the kitchen table. Then my husband begins to read. We've all cried through *Old Yeller* and laughed through *Uncle Remus*. Our hearts have been warmed by the Little House books. Sometimes the kids act out the story we are reading. This part of our evening has become a celebration, pulling together our six personalities. As we respond with laughter or with tears to the story and to each other, we feel warm and cozy. We belong to each other.

In the week ahead, select three evenings when you can gather around the kitchen table. Choose a favorite book or a fun game to play. Serve a special snack. And celebrate your family.

19 Hardships:
The Bumpy Ride

Adult Reflection

In 1992 the recession hit our family. My husband, who is presently an assistant principal for middle-school children, was cut from his position along with eleven other school administrators. We struggled through the first summer, and Phil was able to land another position. The catch is that his position is in a city over three hundred miles from us! For almost two years we have tried simultaneously to sell our home so we can be with Phil and to look for jobs here so he can be with us, but neither has worked out.

Without choice or warning I am on my own with two children, a home, a full-time job and an uncertain future. Without choice or warning Phil is leading a solitary life, empty of children and their passages and empty of my companionship and support. These past two years can only be described as a journey, complete with a roller-coaster ride of emotions each day.

When the worst moments come, late at night after the kids are in bed, or Sundays after Phil has managed to come home for the week-end and is leaving again, a gentle, caring voice reminds me of several of my friends: Peggy, whose husband died unexpectedly this past year, and Scott, who is struggling through an embittered divorce. This does not invalidate my feelings, but it puts my situation into perspective, reminding me to cherish the good stuff in a crummy circumstance, and perhaps most importantly to reach out to those around me with the comforting arm of one who is willing to share a seat on the roller coaster.

God and I have ongoing, passionate dialogues. Through the roller-coaster rides of "why, when, how," and "now, Lord?" I have come to be convinced of his abiding love and care. But most of all I have learned that I do not follow Jesus because he ensures protection from hardships, disappointments, failures or heartaches. I follow Jesus because he is Lord.

Family Reflection

Sometimes when things get really hard or we are tired from trying, we are tempted to give up. Why can Erin get an A on her test without even studying? Why am I the only one who has to take out the trash? It doesn't seem fair when others' lives seem to be going smoothly and ours is a bumpy ride.

Sometimes life is hard. So we feel bad and hope for a good day soon. When the good day comes, not only does it feel wonderful, but we have some experience to help our friends when their life is hard. God gave us our lives and God loves us very much. He never promised that nothing would ever go wrong, but he has definitely promised that he will always love us and be with us no matter what.

Day 1. Israel Suffers in Egypt. Exodus 1:1-22.
1. Why did the Egyptians fear the Hebrew people?
2. In other countries and in our own country, where do you see people disliking and mistreating those of a different race?

Day 2. The People Confess Their Sins. Nehemiah 9:1-3, 32-37.
As the Hebrews have returned from their exile, Nehemiah courageously leads them. His two main concerns: the rebuilding of the temple and the faithful recovery of the Law and its interpretation.
1. In their confession, what do the Hebrew people say is the cause of their hardships?
2. What part, if any, do you think you have played in creating some of the struggles you are now facing?

Day 3. God Responds to Job. Job 38:1-6, 31-36, 26-30; 40:1-5.
The story of Job is not meant to answer the question, Why do good people suffer? Rather, it shows faith in the face of suffering and hardships. Job has encountered terrible trauma and tragedies. In order to justify himself he must condemn God. This, then, is part of God's response.
1. How does Job think of himself after God answers him?
2. What do you think is the most awesome thing that God has done?

Day 4. Those Who Trust God. Psalm 91.
1. In what way will God protect and keep you?
2. Hard times can make us feel anxious and afraid. Is that happening to you? Talk about the things that most frighten you about your situation.

Day 5. A Paralytic Is Brought to Jesus. Mark 2:1-13.
1. How is the paralyzed man able to make his way to see Jesus?
2. Sometimes our situations seem hopeless to us. Name four people you feel you can count on for help and encouragement. What difference do they make for you?

Day 6. Bent and Doubled, a Woman Is Healed. Luke 13:10-17.
1. Jesus had done a wonderful thing. Why were the synagogue officials upset?
2. We are often frustrated with God's timing in meeting our needs. Think of a time when God's timing, although frustrating at the moment, proved to be best after all.

20 Marriage:
Heart and Soul

Adult Reflection

Ancient Hebrew tradition taught that God has created a soulmate for each of us. When questioned about broken relationships, one rabbi replied that marriages break because the partners were not discerning and patient enough to wait until they discovered their true destiny. Another view is that with a great investment of time, energy and commitment, any marriage can bloom into a relationship with depth and texture beyond our wildest imaginings.

Whichever way you view finding your true love, it is indeed a miracle that in this world teeming with people and diversity, we are still able to connect in a way that is deep and pure and bursting with hope and promise.

Marriage is based on trust. "I will give my heart and soul to you, and I trust you to guard and cherish them and never use them against me." Perhaps that is one of the reasons the Bible refers to the church with such intimacy as the "bride of Christ." We come together with hope and promises to give ourselves to each other totally—at least that is our attempt. Love and commitment are risky at times, but the greatest risk comes with being unwilling to risk. Love without commitment is a tragedy. Love with commitment is a marriage.

Family Reflection

Marriage is like having a best friend. Some days you want to be together every minute, and other days you feel tired and want to be apart. There is joy and laughter, anger and tears. It is so wonderful and at the same time *so* much work! God loves us deeply, and one way he can help us to understand his love is through marriage. In marriage the Bible tells us that we are to treat each other the same way Christ treats us—with love, respect, dignity and commitment.

Day 1. The First Marriage. Genesis 2:18-25.

1. What reason does God give that we should leave our parents and homes to marry?

2. Parents, talk about what it was like when you left home. In biblical days women usually left their family only in order to marry. Times and traditions have changed. Discuss some of these changes.

Day 2. Time to Be Together. Deuteronomy 24:5.

1. What were newly married men excused from?

2. How do you make sure you spend quality time with the people you love?

Day 3. Boaz Marries Ruth. Ruth 4:1-18.

Ruth has returned with her mother-in-law, Naomi, to Naomi's homeland. Ruth's husband has died, and the two women are left struggling for food. The custom of that day was that the next of kin would marry the widow and care for her. Boaz is not the next of kin but has fallen in love with Ruth and now seeks through the proper ways to make her his wife.

1. How is Boaz able to have Ruth for his wife?

2. These traditions may seem strange to us today. What are some traditions of marriage and weddings that come to your mind? Share some memories from the last wedding you attended—or from your own.

Day 4. Mary and Joseph. Matthew 1:18-1.
1. Why did Joseph go ahead with his engagement to Mary?
2. Things are not always as they appear. Try to think of an event in your community or in the world where the first news out was not accurate or true.

Day 5. Marriage in Heaven. Matthew 22:23-40.
1. Jesus tells the Sadducees that they are wrong. What does he say are the reasons for their mistake?
2. What are five of the best reasons you can think of to be married?

Day 6. Love as Christ Loves. Ephesians 5:1-2, 21-33.
1. What reason does Paul give that husband and wife should be subject to one another?
2. In what ways are each member of your family responsible for one another—husband for wife, wife for husband, parents for children, children for parents, brothers and sisters for one another?

How can you better take care of one another?

21 Sexuality:
God's Good Gift

What is the first question you ask after hearing about the birth of a baby? Chances are you don't ask its name, weight or length, or how the mother is doing. Probably your first question is, Is it a boy or a girl?

Our sexuality is the crossroads wherein our souls, minds and bodies meet. During adolescence, they not only meet but collide—much like a train hitting a car on the tracks at 110 miles per hour! Whether you believe it is innate, learned or ten thousand years' worth of culture, our sexuality celebrates our distinctiveness as male and female, our differences and the humanness we share. Our sexuality represents the very essence of who we are.

We are constantly trying to define and understand this part of ourselves. The problem is that often we approach sexuality much as a baby might approach the family cat. Babies cannot understand the fragility of a living creature or the notion of causing pain. And so we see the baby pulling the cat's tail, poking its eyes, choking, prodding and inspecting it, until finally the cat will run terrified from the room at the very sight of the child.

God has given us sexuality as a gift to be celebrated with all we set out to do with our lives and the way we relate to the world. We must not shrink it down to the clothes and perfume or cologne we wear or how we walk and talk. God has given us a *good* gift, but just as with any other gift, we can receive it, reject it or abuse it.

Family Reflection

Boys and girls *are* different. The differences show up in all kinds of ways. Certainly there are differences in the way we look, but that's just the beginning!

But wait a minute, isn't everyone different? You and your best friend certainly aren't exactly the same. You like hot dogs but he likes pizza. You like swimming, but she would rather ride bikes. But what about the things that make you best friends— kindness, laughter, trust? Those things make the differences easier to handle.

God made you a very special person. You are a boy or a girl, and wherever you go you can bring that gift with you! You have a special way of thinking, problem solving, understanding and being a good friend. Your sexuality is much more than what your body looks like and can do; it is a celebration of who you are, and it is a *good* gift from God.

Day 1. Created in God's Image. Genesis 1:26-31.
1. What did God command men and women to do after he created them?
2. Human beings rule the earth. What are some negative things we have done?

What are some positive things?

Day 2. God Has Formed Us. Psalm 139:13-18.
1. What reason does the psalmist give for giving God thanks?
2. God makes good stuff. List three things that you think are good about each member of your family.

Day 3. Brought from Death to Life. Romans 6:5-14.
1. How can we no longer be slaves to sin?
2. What do you think are some of the hardest things about being male or female?

Day 4. Our Bodies, Temples of the Holy Spirit. 1 Corinthians 6:19-20.

1. Why does Paul say we are not our own?

2. *Glorify* means to bring honor and help others to respect God. What are some things you do with your body that glorify God?

What are some things you do with your body that don't glorify God?

Day 5. Ancient Male and Female Traditions. 1 Corinthians 11:1-16.

Paul is encouraging the Corinthian church to treasure their sexuality and mark those differences with the customs of the time. Scholars speculate that in their new-found freedom in Christ, some Corinthians were trying to dissolve the sexual barriers; women were shaving their heads and dressing as men, men were adorning themselves as women.

1. In what way does Paul say men and women are dependent on one another?

2. Talk about traditions for men and women in the past and present. (How have things changed? What things seem to have stayed the same? What do you think might happen in the future?)

Day 6. We Are One in Christ. Galatians 3:23-29.

1. In what way have we all become one?

2. Think of a person with whom you are having trouble getting along, and describe that person with three words.

Now try to see him or her as though you were Jesus looking at them. Choose three words that you think Jesus might use to describe them.

Was there any difference? If so, why?

Special Activity: Kids' Night Out

My daughter Jillian loves to ice skate. So one night she and I invited one of her friends to join us for a girls' night out. Leaving her three brothers behind, we enjoyed a cozy dinner together, and then the fun began as she taught me how to skate. Sometimes it's fun for it to be "just us girls."

If possible, plan a girls' night out and a boys' night out with your family for the coming week. If it won't work to do it that way, let the males choose an activity one evening and the females another evening. Enjoy the special bond that exists with those of your own gender, while appreciating the differences in the other.

22 Teaching:
Walking the Talk

For the Adult

My friend Yerta, age eighty-three, ministered to patients in our Alzheimer's center and occasionally helped in our church nursery. One day in my office I was telling her my concerns about my oldest child, Sarah. Sarah is such a perfectionist that she sometimes makes impossible demands on herself. Good grades, model student, student council leader—all things to be happy about, yet I was afraid that Sarah was missing out on the simple things, like dreaming, wishing, exploring, waiting. After I finished speaking, Yerta looked around the room at my diplomas and my heaping desk, covered with projects, and said, "The apple doesn't fall far from the tree."

Teaching our children doesn't mean pouring information into their heads. It means being an active participant in their transformation as well as our own. We cannot stand at a distance from them and say, "Now you listen to me and do as I say." It isn't enough that we know what to do and say; we must also have the courage and desire to live out what we believe.

On one level teaching means to equip our children with the knowledge and skill that they will need to move forward as citizens of this world and as children of the kingdom. On another level teaching means that through example and experience our children find the internal desire to live in the peace and potential that are their birthright as children of God.

Family Reflection

If you were trying to learn how to blow a huge bubble or hit a line drive, who would be the best person to teach you?

Wouldn't it be helpful if the person teaching you could actually show you? Those are examples of things that we *do,* but we also learn things about *who we are* by the way we are treated and by the way we see others being treated. If you have a baby sister or brother or maybe even a baby cousin or neighbor, you'll find that quite quickly they begin to imitate everything you do. They will try to dress, walk, talk and act exactly like you. That makes you very responsible for the way you behave when you are around them. That makes you a teacher!

Day 1. Teach Them God's Words. Deuteronomy 11:1, 18-21.
1. When is the right time to teach the ways of the Lord?
2. Who teaches you about your faith?

Day 2. Teach the Wonders of God. Psalm 78:1-8.
1. What law did God appoint in Israel?
2. If there was just one thing you could tell someone about God, what would that be?

Pick a person you would like to share this with—maybe through a letter, a telephone call or face to face. Tell your family about your plan.

Day 3. Jesus Feeds the Five Thousand. Matthew 14:13-21.
Jesus has just been given the news that his cousin John the Baptist was beheaded for his outspokenness in calling Herod the tetrarch to repentance.
1. Why did Jesus want to feed the people who followed him?
2. Name someone who looks up to you. How do you care for him or her?

Day 4. Jesus' Last Commandment. Matthew 28:1-20.
1. What does Jesus ask his disciples to do after he is gone? What

promise does he give along with the command?

2. Teaching isn't just saying something, it is living it. Think about the way you act and treat other people. What might people learn about Christ from the way you lead your life?

Day 5. Jesus Teaches God's Words. John 7:1, 11-18.
1. From where does Jesus say that the things he is teaching are coming?
2. Who do you think Jesus was?

Day 6. The Apostles Are Imprisoned for Teaching. Acts 5:17-42.
The apostles had been filled with the power of the Holy Spirit and were doing acts of wonder and miracles. People throughout Jerusalem were coming to them to hear them teach and preach, and to experience healing.
1. What reason does Peter give for continuing to teach?
2. What pressures keep you from sharing your life in Christ with others?

Part 3
Faith Life

23 Baptism:
Waters of Grace

Adult Reflection

When Jesus came up out of the baptismal waters, Scripture tells us that the first words spoken by God were "This is my son." In a very real sense these words are part of our baptismal experience as well. Baptism is not an action on our part as much as a reaction to God's action. God makes the first move toward us in grace, and we move toward God in response.

Baptism is a mystery. No matter how much we think we understand the sacraments historically or theologically, God in his infinite wisdom has reserved a portion that we simply cannot explain or understand. The Creator calls us to himself with the intimacy of family, much like the gracious father running down the dirty path toward his prodigal son, tears streaming, arms outstretched, dignity and pride lost, crying out, "My son, my son!"

God calls us to belong to him. We are claimed as his and given his name. We are given his kingdom and everything in it as our birthright. Perhaps baptism can be likened to the waters that a newborn must pass through to make her entrance into this world. The waters are not only substance for cleansing but a medium for passage, resulting in a new creation.

Family Reflection

When you go to the circus, you might see a magician pulling a dime out of his ear or making a rabbit disappear. This isn't really magic but a very good trick. The magician came up with a way to make you see only what he wanted you to see. Being baptized isn't anything like magic tricks. You don't look any different after you are baptized, and maybe you really don't feel all that different either. The changes really started with God. God loves us so much that he was willing to die for us. And so he sent his son, Jesus, to make sure we could always be very close to God, like a family should be. God said "I love you" by sending Jesus. We say "I love you back" when we are baptized.

Day 1. John Baptizes Jesus. Matthew 3.
1. Why didn't John want to baptize Jesus?
2. Talk about your own baptism or one you have witnessed. What is the one thing that stands out for you about that experience?

Day 2. Baptism of the Holy Spirit. Acts 1:1-11.
1. What things did Jesus promise that the Holy Spirit would give his apostles the power to do?
2. What places do you feel most uncomfortable sharing your faith? Why?
Where do you feel most comfortable and natural talking about God? Why?

Day 3. Baptisms in the First Church. Acts 2:29-47.
1. Those who had heard the message about Jesus asked what they should do. How did Peter respond?
2. When was the first time you really heard the story of Jesus? Who shared this message with you?

Day 4. Paul Tells His Story. Acts 22:1-16.
1. What reason did Ananias give for Paul's experience on the road to Damascus?
2. Who has helped you to better understand your relationship

with God? How did they go about doing this?

Day 5. Baptized in Christ. 1 Corinthians 1:10-17.
1. What kinds of quarrels were reported by Chloe's people?
2. Sometimes we rely on our church leaders to do our spiritual work (like worship, Sunday school, Bible studies). What do you do for yourself to help your relationship with God grow?

Day 6. One Baptism. Ephesians 4:1-7.
1. How does Paul tell us we should live our lives?
2. What are some differences in the ways people you know follow God?

24 Christian:
What's in a Name?

Adult Reflection

In ancient times, and for a very long time after, people had no official last names. What they did have were titles to indicate what tribe they were from or whose son or daughter they were. Later this would include what the parents did for an occupation—smith, cook, potter, weaver. Such names connected people to a broader community and gave individuals a collective as well as a personal identity. Names communicated not only *who one was* but also to *whom one belonged.* It works the same for those who call themselves Christian. The name *Christian* is not so much an indication of what we do as a sweet confession of to whom we belong.

Family Reflection

Christian means Christ-follower, but following Jesus is much more than playing follow the leader with your best friend at recess. When we play follow the leader we don't really think about what we are doing. The important part is to do exactly what the leader does, until it's your turn to lead. As Christians, however, we don't just do exactly what Christ our leader does; we want to *belong* to him. We want to be such a part of him that we can never be apart from him.

Day 1. The Church at Antioch. Acts 11:19-30.

Jesus has been crucified and resurrected. He has appeared to many and taken leave of his disciples before ascending into heaven. Peter has had a vision that instructed him to spread the gospel to the Gentiles. Many of those who were following Jesus and his disciples were being persecuted.

1. Who did Barnabas bring to Antioch and why?

2. What do you like best about your church?

What things would you like to change?

Day 2. A Christian's Walk. Ephesians 4:17-20, 25-32.

1. What is the reason Paul gives that we should speak truth, each one of us, with our neighbor?

2. Is there someone you are not getting along with? Write that person's name on a slip of paper, trade slips, and take turns praying for them. Pray also that you will be able to forgive that person and be reconciled.

Day 3. Treat Each Other with Christian Love. Romans 12:10-18.

1. How are we to think of ourselves?

2. Think of someone who always seems to put you first. What does that person do that makes you feel they put you first?

Day 4. Rejoice in the Lord. Philippians 4:4-9.

1. With what things are we encouraged to fill our minds?

2. What things do you enjoy thinking about?

What kinds of thoughts bother you? How could you change your thoughts?

Day 5. Putting on a New Self. Colossians 3:1-17.

1. What changes will being renewed in Christ bring?

2. If you could change two things about yourself, what would they be?

Name two things you like about yourself and would never want to change.

Day 6. Living up to Our New Name. 1 Thessalonians 5:12-28.
1. What do these Scriptures tell us is God's will for our lives in Christ Jesus?
2. Tell about several events from the past year for which you are most thankful.

Special Activity: New Names
The other morning I was grouchy and mean to my son Kyle. I was running late, and in a rude way I had taken out my tension on my son. I felt terrible about it later. When Kyle got home from school, I apologized to him. He showed me great mercy. "Mom, sometimes I get mean when I'm in a hurry too. It's okay." His forgiveness felt wonderful. If I had to give Kyle a new name that reflected the Christian character I saw in him that day, I might call him "Forgiver and Shower of Mercy."

What Christian character traits do you see in the members of your family? How have you touched each other's lives with the love of Christ? Give everyone a paper placemat to decorate for another family member. Give the person whose placemat you are decorating a new name—a name that reflects his or her faith. Write the name on the placemat, and draw pictures to illustrate the new name. Enjoy eating meals on your new placemats. You may want to cover them with clear contact paper to preserve them.

25 Communion:
Memory and Mystery

Adult Reflection

Communion, commune, community, communist and *communication* are all words that share the same root. Within their definitions you will find literally and implied, coming together, oneness, connection. Yet this oneness does not mean only the actual physical sense of being together but a sense of sharing space and heart, struggle and joy. There is a built-in vulnerability and a strength and a presence.

When Jesus took the elements of the traditional Jewish Passover and gave them new meaning, he put his very life on the line. Had he not done so, our lives would have been forfeited. When Jesus says, "Do this in remembrance of me," we are invited to come together as one with each other and with Christ. We come together in shared space and heart, struggle and joy, vulnerability and strength, to celebrate and remember *his* presence.

Family Reflection

What kinds of things do you use to remember special people, dates or events? Perhaps you use a calendar for special dates or a keepsake box for letters and photographs. I'll bet there are certain songs or smells that instantly make you remember a special time in your life. For me, the smell of watermelon always reminds me of the first day of summer vacation when I was in the third grade.

When we share Communion in church, we are remembering. But we aren't just remembering something that happened long ago. We are remembering that God gave us each other to love and take care of. We are remembering how God loved us so much that he sent his Son, Jesus, to die for us and to live again . . . for us! We are also remembering that Jesus is with us even now.

Why don't we use bananas and apple juice instead of bread and grape juice or wine? Because Jesus used the food that was on his table as he celebrated the ancient Jewish tradition of Passover. When Jesus came to the bread and wine, he said, "Every time you come together, eat this and remember me." So that is what we do.

Day 1. The Passover Feast. Exodus 12:1-14, 24-28.

God had sent Moses to free the Hebrew people from slavery in Egypt. The killing of the firstborn was the final event in a series of plagues meant to convince the pharaoh of Egypt to let the people of God go free and return to their homeland.

1. Why did God have the Hebrew people mark their door frames with blood?

2. The Hebrew people were told to celebrate this feast every year from that day on in order to remember what God had done for them. What kinds of celebrations do Christians have to remind us of the wonderful things that God has done for us?

Day 2. The Last Supper. Luke 22:1-23.

1. What new meaning does Jesus give the Passover wine?

2. Jesus was preparing himself and his disciples for the events that were about to take place. Talk about some goals you have as a family and how you are working toward those goals.

Day 3. Jesus Is the Bread of Life. John 6:26-40.

Jesus has just performed the miracle of feeding the five thousand people who had come to hear his teachings and to seek healing.

1. What does Jesus describe as "the work of God"?

2. Play a game together where each person takes a turn and says one thing they know about Jesus. Keep going until you can't think of anything to add. Then sum up all of the things that were listed.

Day 4. The Early Church Practices the Lord's Supper. Acts 2:41-47.

This follows the Pentecost experience in which the people who had gathered were filled with the Holy Spirit and thousands became believers in Jesus as the Christ.

1. What did the early Christians do every day?

2. In what ways is your life the same as and different from the description of the lives of the early Christians?

Day 5. The Bread and Cup of Unity. 1 Corinthians 10:14-11:1.

Paul is trying to guide the Corinthian church to a balance in their participation with the surrounding community. He urges them to be free from the strict Jewish dietary laws but not to go so far as to participate in pagan religious rituals.

1. What does Paul say should be the goal of everything we do?

2. Being sensitive to others' beliefs is an ancient Christian tradition. When have you needed to be sensitive to others' beliefs? (Perhaps you have had guests who required vegetarian or kosher foods, or you may have had to deal with strong feelings about the use of alcohol.)

Day 6. The Proper Attitude for Sharing the Lord's Supper. 1 Corinthians 11:17-28.

1. What were some of the members of the early church doing when they met together and shared the Lord's Supper?

2. Our Communion traditions are far different from the early church tradition of an actual meal. Talk about the tradition of your church. What do you like best about it and what things do you think could be improved?

Special Activity: Family Communion

When my grandmother was in her eighties, she developed terminal cancer. I will never forget the last Sunday she was able to be out of bed. She called all of the family together, and we took Communion in the living room. Never had the words "For whenever you eat this bread and drink this cup, you proclaim the Lord's death until he comes" had more meaning, for we all knew that he would be coming very soon for my grandma. Even today, when I take Communion I like to picture my grandmother in heaven, dining at the banquet table of the King! Communion offers us an opportunity to participate in the timelessness of Jesus.

Gather your family together for a Communion service. You can use your own saltine crackers and grape juice. Allow everyone to participate by saying a prayer, reading a Scripture verse or passing out the crackers and juice. Give everyone an opportunity to share a little bit of what Jesus means and what your family means to them. Think about how wonderful it will be when Jesus comes again.

26 Demons:
The Shadowlands

Adult Reflection

Human beings have the potential for evil just as they have the potential for good. Paul talks about doing the things that he does not want to do. Addicts describe feeling driven or compelled to abuse alcohol or food. Whatever the situation, it is a potential we know lives in the shadowlands of our soul. Most people keep this side of themselves as far away from those they love as possible, and far away from the way they live every day.

The subject of demons is a tricky one. On the one hand we acknowledge that there are forces we know little about and quite frankly find frightening at times. On the other hand we cannot let go of ultimate responsibility and accountability for our own lives and actions. On more than one occasion Jesus dealt with the problem with forgiveness. This drove the religious leaders crazy! To cast out supernatural beings from the netherworld is one thing, but to step into God's territory, the human heart and soul, and offer forgiveness and comfort and peace is quite another.

All definitions and explanations agree that demons are inferior to God. Jesus took authority over evil and empowered us to do the same. And the same treatment Jesus used can most certainly be effective today. Jesus healed people afflicted with demons. He healed them with forgiveness and an outstretched hand.

Family Reflection

We know that evil exists in the world. We see and hear about things people do that are scary and confusing. Sometimes we don't understand why we do some of the things we do. When we talk about demons, we are talking about forces that keep us from having the best possible relationship with God. The most important thing to remember about demons is that they are less powerful than God. That means that God can help you and protect you and keep you safe. But you have to make some choices yourself and decide what kind of person you would like to be.

Day 1. Jesus Begins His Ministry. Matthew 4:12-17, 23-25.
The John this passage refers to is the cousin of Jesus commonly known as John the Baptist.
1. What were the three things Jesus was doing in Galilee?
2. If Jesus were to appear at the baseball field in your town, who would you take to have healed and why?

Day 2. The Pharisees Doubt the Spirit of Jesus. Matthew 12:22-30.
1. What does Jesus say happens when a kingdom does not stand united?
2. Have you ever thought that someone was acting nice for the wrong reasons? Tell what happened.

Day 3. The Gerasene Demoniac. Mark 5:1-20.
1. What did Jesus want the man to do after he had been healed?
2. Sometimes we do things that are not good for us and can hurt us. Talk about some of these problems in your life: a dangerous habit, a bad attitude, holding grudges or wanting revenge. Whatever it is, pray for God to heal these things.

Day 4. Mary Magdalene, Follower of Christ. Mark 16:1-13.
1. What makes Mary Magdalene different from Jesus' other followers?

2. Have you ever lost the trust of friends, teachers or family? How did you rebuild that trust? Or how *can* you rebuild trust?

Day 5. The Seventy Disciples Return. Luke 10:17-20.

1. What does Jesus tell his disciples they should rejoice in?

2. Name three things about yourself that you think are most pleasing to God. (Try to avoid things that you do or achievements that you've earned.)

Day 6. Paul and the False Leaders. Acts 19:11-20.

1. Why wasn't the man with the evil spirits healed by the seven sons of the Jewish high priest?

2. Pretending to be something you're not can get you into trouble, or at least make for an uncomfortable situation. Have you ever spoken or acted in a way that you did not really believe was right?

27 Disciples:
Follow the Leader

Adult Reflection

Jesus has a hard message to share with those who would choose to follow him. He talks of going out as a sheep among wolves, of being careful, shrewd and discerning. Jesus doesn't soften the call with words like *if* or *perhaps* when he speaks of being persecuted and oppressed. Jesus says, *"When* you are persecuted . . ."* The implication is that struggle and hardship, even suffering, are part of the package marked "disciple."

The word *disciple* may prompt us automatically to think of the apostles. We may think of the image of the apostles that was handed down through the Middle Ages—gallant, noble men, free from blemish (and, frankly, completely free of their humanity), bearing a righteous message that came to them word-for-word from God. Scripture, however, shows disciples who were poorly educated and prone to internal bickering and insufferable arrogance, men who quite often missed the meaning of Jesus' words and actions and misread his intentions.

Jesus chose to rest the salvation of the world and his own mission on the shoulders of people who were not necessarily religious or even bright. But these were people who brought their callused hands and hearts, without question, to the adventure they were called to by Jesus. They were willing to surrender themselves unconditionally and walk (with fear and trembling) into the fire. The band of disciples grew to include men, women and children. Each was called and moved by the power of God who became a man because of an unquenchable love for us.

Family Reflection

What do Simon Peter, Andrew, James and John the sons of Zebedee, Philip, Bartholomew, Thomas, Matthew, James the son of Alphaeus, Thaddaeus, Simon the Zealot (insert your name and the names of your family members here) and Judas Iscariot all have in common? You might have thought you knew until you heard your name in the middle of all those others. But you were right anyway. They are all disciples!

When we love Jesus and choose to live in a way that shows the whole world how much we love him, we are on our way to being his disciples. When we can turn around and help other people to know how much Jesus loves them, we really are disciples.

Day 1. The Twelve Disciples Are Instructed for Service. Matthew 10:1-20.

1. What was the main message the disciples were instructed to give to the people of Israel?

2. What instructions would you give for living as a disciple of Christ today?

Day 2. Responsible Behavior for Disciples. Matthew 18:1-7.

1. Why did Jesus tell his disciples that they must become like children?

2. A stumbling block is something that gets in your way and can stop you from getting to where you want to go. What is a stumbling block for you in your relationship with God, with your family or with a friend?

Day 3. Jesus Appears at the Sea of Galilee. John 21:1-17.

Jesus has been crucified and is now seen after his resurrection.

1. When did the disciples know it was Jesus standing on the shore?

2. In what ways do you recognize Christ in other people?

Day 4. Seventy Disciples Are Sent Out. Luke 10:1-17.
1. When the disciples were rejected, who did Jesus say was really being rejected?
2. Tell about a time that you felt rejected by a person or a group.

Day 5. Mary and Martha. Luke 10:38-42.
1. Why was Martha upset with her sister?
2. Both women are important in this story. Who are you more like, Mary or Martha? Explain.

Day 6. Choosing of the Seven. Acts 6:1-7.
A Hellenistic Jew was a Jew who had adopted the Greek language and, to some extent, Greek customs and culture.
1. What were the seven men, chosen by the twelve apostles, to do?
2. Talk about some of the different ways that people serve God in your church. What is something that each of you might like to do?

Special Activity: Service Project
Plan a special service project for your family to do in the week ahead. Do you know a single parent? Maybe you could offer to babysit one evening. Is there an elderly person in your neighborhood who could use some help with yard work? Could you take a meal to someone who is ill? Is there someone you know who is lonely and would enjoy being invited over for an evening with your family? Whatever you decide to do, use it as an opportunity to show someone else the love of Jesus.

28 Faith:
The Chicken or the Egg?

Adult Reflection

Do we believe because we have faith? Or do we have faith because we believe? We can ponder and wrestle with chicken-egg questions until those chickens come home to roost. But perhaps we would be better off looking at and feeling the texture of faith itself and the One whose actions define faith's essence so beautifully and fully.

If there is one characteristic of God that spills out of the Scriptures, it is God's faithfulness: God's steadfast, unswerving, immovable, cast-in-concrete faithfulness. By God's sheer act of faith in us, we are lifted out of the dust of our creation into a position of steward over all that has been created. We are given the honor of creating life and the responsibility of sustaining it. In story after story from the Bible God continues to have faith in humankind. God disciplines Adam and Eve but continues a relationship with them. Noah and his family are saved to begin a new creation. God sends Jesus because God felt we were worth saving.

So we muddle along with the man who cried out, "Lord, I believe, help me in my unbelief!" How God must have thrown back his head and belly-laughed with delight at this honest and honorable response. And as we live in our own faith-skins perhaps we can be more generous to God and to one another. Perhaps we can see potential and worth without proof or product. With God as our model we can learn to love deeply without weighing or measuring. Because of God's faithfulness, our faith can be steadfast and unsinkable.

Family Reflection

When you go to bed at night do you think you need to pray super hard to make sure that the sun will come up in the morning? Do you worry that the sun will just decide to go dark? Probably not, and the reason is because the sun always comes up. Sure it gets covered up by clouds and goes through an eclipse now and then, but we know it's still there! So we have faith in the sun because the sun is faithful. That's the first part of having faith in God.

The second part is about knowing. For example, you can't really get inside someone else's head and know what they are thinking, so you can never be 100 percent sure of why someone is your friend. But there is something about the way you feel when you are with that person that makes you know, beyond a shadow of a doubt, that this person is a friend—you like and care about each other. So we have faith in our best friend because we just know we can.

Faith has a lot to do with who or what is the object of your faith, but it also has to do with you. God is like the sun: always there, something you can count on and trust. The difference is that God made the sun, so you can count on God even more. The other part is just knowing, without explanation or reason, that God loves and cares for you. God has faith in you. Think about that!

Day 1. The Walls of Jericho. Joshua 6:1-20.

Jericho is an ancient city in the wide plain where the Jordan Valley broadens between two mountain ranges. It lay on the Israelites' route into Canaan, and they needed to conquer it in order to cross over into the Promised Land.

1. As the Israelites marched around Jericho for six days, they followed a pattern. What did they do differently on the seventh day?

2. The Israelites demonstrated their faith at Jericho through their obedience. In what ways does God expect you to be obedient?

Day 2. Judah Is Invaded by Fierce Enemies. 2 Chronicles 20:1-23.

Jehoshaphat is a righteous king over Judah, the true Israel in the eyes of the chronicler. He has established a justice system for dealing with disputes among the tribes when the enemies of Judah attack.

1. What part do the people of Judah play in the victory battle?

2. Talk about the ways you invite God to help you solve your problems.

Day 3. The Faithfulness of God. Psalm 89:1-18.

1. What two things does the psalmist say make up the foundation of God's throne?

2. What do you consider to be the most awesome part of God's creation?

Day 4. The Centurion's Faith. Matthew 8:5-13.

1. What was so extraordinary about the faith of the centurion?

2. What times in your life have you felt that you did not deserve God's faith in you?

Day 5. Peter's Confession. Matthew 16:13-20.

1. How was Peter's answer to Jesus' question different from the way others had answered?

2. How would you describe Jesus to someone who had never heard of him?

Day 6. The Triumphs of Faith. Hebrews 11:1—12:2.

1. With so many examples of faith, who stands out as the One who perfects faith?

2. If each of you were added to this list, what would be said about your faith?

29 Gifts: *I'm the Surprise!*

Adult Reflection

A gift is something extra—that little something we have had our eye on for some time but could never get for ourselves (or at least never get guilt-free!). Getting the gift is one third of the fun, another third is unwrapping it and holding it in the light, but the final third is really the best—when we actually use our gift. Perhaps we smell better, look ravishing or have an evening of reading to look forward to, but whatever the case, it is now our gift.

Our spiritual gifts are similar. We all have gifts, no matter what our past or present circumstances. But only one third of the fun is in *having* spiritual gifts. When we unwrap and use the gift, then we can fully appreciate it.

When we are affirmed for the gifts we use in serving the Lord, often, with all good intentions, we invalidate the gift: "No, no, please—all the credit must go to the Lord for that beautiful song." Yet the Lord chose *you* to have the gift. What parent would give their child a gift and then snatch it back to open, explaining what incredible, wonderful parents they were for finding such a gift? No, we smile and swallow a lump in our throats when our precious children struggle with the ribbon, their faces glowing with joy and anticipation. And the greatest reward comes when they use the gift and cherish it.

Family Reflection

It's so much fun to see presents in a huge pile on my birthday. I love the shiny paper and bright ribbon and, most of all, the tags on each one with my name on them!

What if all you could do with your gifts was to sit and look at them? Pretty soon you would lose interest and probably be very disappointed, maybe even angry. We love to get gifts, but we really love to open them up and try them out.

Maybe you are really good at drawing, skating, singing, spelling, speaking, dancing, thinking, dreaming, inventing, playing kickball, hopscotch, handball, baseball, soccer, making Lego sculptures, baking cookies, helping others, giving smiles and hugs, printing, writing, typing or finding solutions! (Whew!) Those are only a few of the many gifts that God has given us. But our gifts aren't really any good unless we open and use them.

Day 1. A New Spirit. Ezekiel 11:13-21.

The Hebrew people were scattered out of the Promised Land by foreign hostile nations. The remnant are those who were allowed to remain. These people came to believe that the exiles had borne God's punishment and their property now belonged to those who remained. Ezekiel condemns this and warns them that God is with the exiles and will restore them.

1. What gifts does God promise to give to the exiles when they return?

2. What sad memories do you have in your heart? Stop now and pray for one another, that God might give you the gift from verse 19.

Day 2. Simon the Magician. Acts 8:9-24.

1. How did Simon try to get the gifts of the Holy Spirit?

2. Name five most important things that money cannot buy.

Day 3. Use Your Gifts. Romans 12:1-13.

This letter from Paul closes with ethical teaching and personal remarks in chapters 12—16.

1. According to Paul, how is the gift we are each given decided?

2. Name one thing about yourself that you consider a gift. (If someone has difficulty thinking of one, others can help.)

How could you use your gift even more than you do now?

Day 4. Spiritual Gifts. 1 Corinthians 12.

1. Which gift does Paul consider most important?

2. If you were to compare your gift to a part of your body, which part would it be? Why?

Day 5. The Greatest Gift. 1 Corinthians 13:1-13.

1. If you have all of the gifts but love, what does Paul say that you are left with?

2. List two "good" things that you spend time doing. Why do you do them?

Day 6. Every Good Gift. James 1:12-22.

This is actually a sermon in the form of a letter and is written to a Christian audience, reminding them how Christians ought to live.

1. Where does "every perfect gift" come from?

2. Have you ever asked yourself, "Why is God doing this?" when bad things happen in your life? How do these verses help you to answer that question?

Special Activity: Giving Gifts

What gifts has God given the members of your family? Consider the lists that appear in Romans 12 and 1 Corinthians 12. Also think about the greatest gift, the gift of love. On separate slips of paper, write down one gift you see in each person. Attach a ribbon or bow to each slip of paper. As you share with each person the gift you see, give him or her the paper with the ribbon attached. When you are finished, decorate each person's chair at the dinner table with his or her bows, as a reminder that you are each a wonderful gift from God.

30 God
Creator to Creature

Adult Reflection

O God of promises kept,

How well you know me inside and out. In you there are no false images to maintain. I am truly me in your presence.

You love me with a tenderness that cradles my soul gently next to the soft beating of your heart. I can scarcely take it in! And yet I am not surprised. Are you not the source of all tenderness and the author of cherished moments?

My mind is weary and restless with the demands of the day. Yet here we are together. Your presence is like a soothing balm on a worry-filled forehead.

O Lord, there is no breath drawn, no sight beheld, that does not point to and adore your presence as the Holy Creator. How is it that you in all your glory would steal gently to my side in love and sighs, children and family, work and play?

How is it that you would pursue me into the darkest corners of my heart, mind and intentions? Do you love me so deeply? Gentle Love, I am humbled by your humility and your glory. I am awestruck at your ways, faithful and constant.

I give my whole self to you . . . in part because as a creature to my Creator I can do no less. But sweet Lord, you have made your arms a safe place to be. I give myself to you because you want me. No one has ever wanted me enough to die for me. With you there is no risk of rejection, measure of my worth by my product or disapproval flashing from your eyes.

O God, you are welcoming, and so, Lord, you are welcome. O how I love you, dear God, because you first loved me.

Amen.

Family Reflection

Maybe you talk to God all of the time. Maybe you have never thought about it. Here is a simple prayer for you to use when you can't think of any words.

God, with your warmth and your touch
You love me so much,
Thanks a lot.

For birds and trees and the summer breeze
Thanks a lot.

For fish and fowl and the hooting owl
Thanks a lot.

For nighttime and day, at school and at play,
Thanks a lot.

Amen

Day 1. God's Imagination. Genesis 1:1—2:3.
1. How did God feel about everything that had been created?
2. What would you create today if you had the power? Why?

Day 2. The Holiness of God. Exodus 3:1-15.
Moses has fled Egypt after killing an Egyptian and being hunted for murder by Pharaoh. He has settled in the land of Midian with Jethro and married Jethro's daughter Zipporah.
1. What name does God wish to be remembered by from generation to generation? How does God's name describe God?
2. If one word or phrase could describe you, what would it be?

Day 3. God's Commandment. Deuteronomy 6:1-9.

1. What is the commandment that needs to be repeated over and over again?

2. If you could truly follow this commandment, how might your life be different?

Day 4. God's Ways and Thoughts. Isaiah 55:1-13.

This is a hymn of joy and triumph that celebrates the approaching restoration of Israel.

1. How are God's ways and thoughts different from ours?

2. Think of a situation in your community, your nation or the world where there is violence between two groups of people. Talk about how you feel about each group. How do you think God feels about the situation? Pray for both groups, for reconciliation and healing.

Day 5. God Becomes Human. John 1:1-18.

1. Since no one has ever seen God, how did God become known to us?

2. In what ways do people know God by knowing you?

Day 6. The Love of God. 1 John 4:7-21.

1. Why do we love?

2. How do you show people love?
   What things make you feel loved?

31 Grace:
The Dance

Adult Reflection

The grace, skill and artistry of Fred Astaire made his partners feel and look equally beautiful and talented. As the music played, he led some of the most stunning women of the silver screen into a world where gravity could be wooed and air could become a stairway to the stars. Ballroom dance reveals a lovely irony: the better the leading partner is at his job, the less the other dancer feels that she is being led! And this is like God's work of grace.

When the music of creation began, God, in a movement that can only be described as graceful, moved toward humanity, and we were swept into a relationship. We stumbled along behind, yet there was a beauty, a wonder, in our movements that had everything to do with the leading partner. Time after time, throughout the whole groaning, yearning history of humankind, God has made the first move toward us. Never faltering, never running away from our bumbling steps, God moved closer and closer to us, until one day God could touch us, laugh with us, even share a meal with us.

Grace has nothing to do with who we are and everything to do with who God is. The music began, and God became the Lord of the Dance. In an act of immense tenderness and passion God moved across the floor, reached out a hand and chose us to dance the dance of life.

Family Reflection

When God created the world, it was like a dance. The very first move was when God made us. We stumbled a bit, and sin came into the world. But God took another step toward us, and another, and another, until God was close enough to touch us and be touched by us. That happened when God came to earth as Jesus.

It's really kind of neat if you stop and think about it. God takes one step toward us and we follow the lead—we take one step toward God. God's head is thrown back with a wonderful laugh; as God takes a couple of side steps, we grin and sidestep closer God chose us to be partners because that's the way God wanted it. God has already made the first move; now it's your turn.

Day 1. The Rainbow, a Promise of Grace. Genesis 9:1-17.

Human beings had become so wicked to each other and to the world that God destroyed the world with a flood. The only ones saved were Noah and his family and the animals he brought to the ark. God then made a promise that is a renewal of the promise made at creation.

1. What does God say that he will remember when he sees the bow in the sky?

2. What part of nature reminds you the most of God's love and greatness?

Day 2. Zacchaeus Is Changed by Grace. Luke 19:1-10.

Jericho was on a main trade route and was an important trade center. Zacchaeus, who was a Jew, worked for the Roman government as a tax collector. He was hated and despised by the Jews as a traitor and a corrupt official.

1. What changes did Zacchaeus promise to make and why?

2. What kind of changes have you made as a result of Jesus coming into your life?

Day 3. The Grace of Jesus. Luke 23:32-49.

Jesus has been betrayed by Judas and sentenced to die on the cross. Led to Golgotha, he is crucified.

1. According to these verses, what were the three final acts of Jesus before he died?

2. How do you feel about people you think have treated you unfairly?

Day 4. Tradition and Grace. Acts 15:1-12.

1. Before Jesus, what did the Jewish people do to identify themselves as the chosen people?

How did that requirement change?

2. What has identified you as a child of God?

Day 5. Saved by Grace. Ephesians 2:4-10.

1. What did we do in order to be saved?

2. Paul says that we were created "to do good works." When do you feel you're doing exactly what you were made to do?

Day 6. Grace Is Abundant. 1 Timothy 1:12-17. Paul is reflecting on his life before Christ as Saul the persecutor.

1. What saying does Paul cite as one that is "sure and worthy of full acceptance"?

2. Take turns saying how you were able to see the love and patience of Jesus in one another. "I saw the love and patience of Matthew when . . ."

32 Healing:
A Balm in Gilead

Adult Reflection

My life was a race. I was attending seminary, working full time in the church, mothering two small children and writing my first book. I was juggling as much as I could and finding very little joy in any of it. In the midst of it all I went to a professional conference, thinking that if I just had a vacation and a rest I would be able to pick up where I had left off.

At one Sunday-morning service during the conference an older man in the choir sang "There Is a Balm in Gilead." Looking into his weathered face, I knew he meant it. He had been there. My heart opened to God, and I began reflecting on all that I had been learning and experiencing. What I discovered was that it wasn't a vacation that would put my scattered life back on track; what I needed was *healing*. Jesus was ready to provide it.

Family Reflection

When I was growing up, we had a daily routine to keep things running smoothly at home. But all that would change when one of us was sick. What I remember about being sick is the cool hand of my mom checking my forehead, the noises in her stomach as I lay with my head in her lap, and my dad checking on me as soon as he got home from work. Their love and care helped me to be well. There are many stories in the Bible about the way the angels and Jesus healed people. God loves and cares about us in many different ways and through many different people. Caring is where healing begins.

Day 1. Elijah, Healed from Despair. 1 Kings 19:1-8.
The prophet Elijah has had a remarkable encounter with the prophets of the pagan god Baal. A test on Mount Carmel has proved that the Hebrew God is the only God. Elijah has killed the prophets of Baal, and Queen Jezebel has vowed to do the same to Elijah.
1. Why did Elijah sit down under the juniper tree?
2. Did you ever give up because what you had to do seemed too hard or too risky? Tell what happened.

Day 2. The Lord Heals the Brokenhearted. Psalm 147:1-6.
1. What does it mean for you that God has counted and named the stars?
2. What does the term *brokenhearted* mean?

Can you think of people in your community and in the world who might be brokenhearted? What can your family do to help bring God's healing to these people in need?

Day 3. A Paralytic Cured. Matthew 9:1-8.
1. Why did Jesus have the paralytic rise up and walk?
2. What things do you want forgiveness for today?

Day 4. Jesus Heals Where the Disciples Cannot. Mark 9:14-29.
1. Describe the scene that Jesus saw as he came upon his disciples, the scribes and the people seeking healing.
2. How would you describe your attitude toward some of the challenges you are facing?

How does your attitude compare to the disciples' attitude?

How does your attitude compare to Jesus' attitude?

Day 5. Jesus Heals Ten Lepers. Luke 17:11-19.

Leprosy was a much-feared disease in biblical times. It affects the skin and vital organs, in its most severe form resulting in mutilation and debilitation. Many skin afflictions were attributed to leprosy when in fact they were not. Those even suspected of having the disease were denied access to the healthy community and were forced to live outside town boundaries, relying on charity—people would set food or clothing down and hurry away.

1. What is the difference between the leper who returned to thank Jesus and the nine who did not?

2. What kinds of diseases or conditions today might create the same kind of fear as leprosy did in biblical times?

Day 6. A Lame Man Is Healed. John 5:2-16.

1. Why had the lame man come to lie down by the waters?

2. Where might we look for healing today?

Special Activity: Encouragement

Write each other notes of encouragement to help in the places each person needs healing. Everyone will need enough paper to write everyone else in the family one note. Your note could be a special picture, a Scripture verse or a written message. Roll the finished notes up like a scroll and provide bandage strips to tape the notes closed. On the outside of each note write the name of the person who should receive it. Put all of the notes inside an empty bandage-strips box. Every day, for as long as the notes last, open one note each. Pray for each other, asking God to use your encouragement as a part of the healing.

33 Jesus:
The Word

Adult Reflection

From the very beginning the Word of God had the power to send the great nothing rolling and tumbling and sparking into creation. In the Genesis account we read over and over again that "God said," and it became our reality.

"God said," and we have day and night, time and calendar, earth, moon, stars, sky, oceans. "God said," and we have plants, fish, birds, animals. "God said" and out of the dust and mud of the riverbanks flesh made in the image of God is lifted up and given the breath of life. And "God said, 'It is good.' "

So when God makes the ultimate act of grace and comes to be with us, it is in keeping with the ancient tradition of creation that he would come as the Word become flesh. And once more the order of the world and our reality were changed forever. We are no longer bound by the rules of natural order, which say that death is the end. From the mouth of God came Jesus, "and the Word became flesh and dwelt among us, full of grace and truth."

Family Reflection

With words of God all of creation came to be. The day and night, sun, moon and stars. The mountains, valleys, deserts and jungles came to life because God said. Because of the word of God we have fishes, snakes, elephants, zebras, monkeys, crocodiles—even the platypus! Because God spoke we have oceans, streams and lakes with birds flying high above our heads. Because God spoke we have you and me. And God said it was all good. God loves us so much, so deeply, that God's love itself became a word. This special love-word was Jesus. Jesus came to help us belong to God. Jesus came because God said.

Day 1. The Birth of Jesus. Matthew 1:18-25.

1. What does the Hebrew word *Emmanuel* mean?

2. In what ways do you believe that God is with us today?

Day 2. Jesus Stays Behind at the Temple. Luke 2:41-52.

1. What was so amazing about the way Jesus acted at the temple?

2. Think of two questions you would ask if you had the chance to meet with a group of religious teachers. Discuss your response.

Day 3. Jesus Begins His Ministry with Baptism. Mark 1:1-20.

1. In what ways were the baptism of John and the baptism of Jesus different?

2. What do you understand your baptism or the baptism of your faith to mean?

How are the baptism of Jesus and your baptism different and the same?

Day 4. Jesus and the Father are One. John 10:22-42.

1. What proof did Jesus offer that he was who he claimed?

2. What proof would you be able to offer that you are a Christian?

Day 5. Jesus Before Pilate. John 18:28-40.

Jesus has been betrayed by Judas. The Jewish religious leaders have told lies to see him killed. Jesus now faces Pilate, a Roman government official.

1. What tradition did Pilate offer the Jewish people as a way of saving Jesus?

2. Describe an experience where you or someone you know was falsely accused of doing something wrong.

What was the worst part of being lied about or accused?

Day 6. Jesus Is Alive. Luke 24:13-53.

Mary Magdalene, Joanna and Mary the mother of James have seen Jesus after the resurrection, but the apostles do not believe them. Finally the disciples encounter Jesus themselves.

1. What is one way Jesus shows the disciples that he is human and not just a spirit?

2. How can you deepen your relationship with Christ?

34 Miracles:
Changes in the Heart

Adult Reflection

One of my professors took great pains to illustrate the differences between a true miracle and a wonderful thing that happens within the laws of nature. Thus, he argued that a small tree growing up through asphalt was really no miracle, nor was a baby being born, nor was breaking down a wall that had divided countries. But I believe his approach takes too much for granted.

I am convinced my professor would have spoken differently had he spent more time gazing into the ocean, holding a baby so close you could feel her warm breath on your neck or fighting for another's right to live with dignity.

God continues to work the miracle of renewing hope and bringing change in what seems at times a hopeless world. The miracles described in the Bible reveal this same intent. As you study the miracles of God and of God through Jesus, consider their intent. What moved God to act? How did God reach out again and again to us and draw us close? How is God reaching out for you today?

Family Reflection

Zacchaeus was a traitor and a thief among his own people. He collected taxes for the Romans, who were the captors of the Jewish people, and he collected more than he was supposed to. But when Jesus saw Zacchaeus up in a tree, he saw more than a crook—he saw someone with worth. Zacchaeus responded to Jesus by saying that he would give back all that he had taken and even more. You can bet that it wasn't just the life of Zacchaeus that would change: all of those people Zacchaeus had treated unfairly were in for a wonderful surprise. There are miracles waiting to happen to each of us as well.

Day 1. Manna from God, a Miracle of Trust and Obedience. Exodus 16:1-30.

1. What was the one thing that the Hebrew people were forbidden to do with the manna? Why?

2. Learning to depend completely on God is difficult and sometimes scary. What areas of your life might change as you learn to trust God more?

Day 2. Changing the Heart of a Prophet. Jonah 1—3.

1. Why didn't Jonah want to go to Nineveh and share God's message?

2. List three people with whom you would like to share the message of God's love. What holds you back?

Day 3. A Miracle Changes the Law. Matthew 12:1-21.

1. Why didn't Jesus just wait until the Sabbath was finished to heal the man's withered hand?

2. What kinds of things hold you back from doing everything you would like to do?

Day 4. The Unclean Spirits Recognize Jesus. Mark 1:14-28.

The spirit was called unclean because the effect of the condition separated people from the worship of God.

1. What did people think about Jesus after this miracle?

2. How does your church help needy people in your town? What does this help teach people about Jesus?

Day 5. Jesus Forgives the Paralytic. Luke 5:17-26.
1. Why did Jesus have the paralyzed man stand up and walk?
2. Do you need God's forgiveness for anything? Pray for one another.

Day 6. Lazarus Is Raised from the Dead. John 11:1-44.
1. Why does Jesus pray aloud to God?
2. The way we act can help others to grow in faith. How do you show God's love to others?

Special Activity: The Miracle of Salvation
Fill a dishpan with clean water and get salt, pepper and dish soap. Sprinkle the salt into the water and say, "God made such a beautiful and perfect world. In the beginning the world was clean and lovely. Adam and Eve enjoyed a perfect relationship with God and with each other."

Sprinkle pepper into the water and say, "But then everything changed. Sin entered the world. People started to disobey God. When that happened everything got messed up. The world became dark and dirty. The world needed a miracle. So God provided a miracle. He chose Mary, a young woman without a husband, and miraculously she became the mother of Jesus, God's own Son. Jesus was a beautiful miracle."

Squirt one drop of dish soap into the pan and watch the pepper move away. Then say, "Jesus changed everything! He changed people's hearts, and he changed their lives. One drop of Jesus' blood was enough to wash away even the worst sin."

35 Parables:
Into Life

Adult Reflection

> Jesus told the crowds all these things in parables; without a parable
> he told them nothing. This was to fulfill what had been spoken
> through the prophet:
> "I will open my mouth to speak
>   in parables;
> I will proclaim what has been
>   hidden from the foundation
>   of the world." (Matthew 13:34-35)

Jesus used parables to communicate a truth about our relationship to
God by laying it alongside an experience the people of his time could
understand. Thus the people were not required to listen to a sermon
on an abstract theological concept but instead heard a story about
everyday life. Jesus' hearers may not have immediately grasped the
moral or theological point of a parable, but the parable's situation was
always immediately recognizable to them. Some of the powerful im-
pact of the parable is lost on us because we do not understand the
customs or mindset of the times.

For example, we have often viewed the parable of the lost coin as
drawing on economic conditions to make its point. We might assume
that a coin such as the woman lost was hard to come by, and that the
story illustrates how we are valued by God. While that may be true, how
would your perception change if you knew that in Jesus' day, when a
woman was married part of her marriage vestment was a band of coins
worn on the head? In today's terms, rather than looking for part of her
savings the woman is searching frantically for a stone fallen out of her
marriage band, something more precious than money could buy.

Jesus talked of fishermen, shepherds and landowners because

those were common occupations in his day. How do we communicate the gospel to the people around us? The parables should spur us to look closely at the way we relate to people and to become creative, relevant and real with our message.

Family Reflection

My favorite book when I was in fifth grade was called *The Wind Blows Free.* I read that book six times during the summer between fifth and sixth grade. I could not get enough of the story. Parts of it seemed to have been written for me alone. Maybe you have read a story or seen a movie or heard a song that was the same for you.

When Jesus used parables to teach people about God, the people felt like he was talking just to them. "How did he know?" they would ask themselves. Sometimes they would get the point of the story and sometimes they wouldn't. The disciples often had to ask Jesus what he meant after they had heard a parable. Still, the parables were meant to make God clearer and easier to understand.

Day 1. Laborers in the Vineyard. Matthew 20:1-16.

1. Why were the laborers who were hired in the morning unhappy with what they got paid?

2. Which group of laborers are most like you and why?

Day 2. The Marriage of the King's Son. Matthew 22:1-14.

1. What reasons were given by those who turned down the king's invitation?

2. What are some of the reasons you might have for not giving yourself fully to God?

Day 3. The Talents. Matthew 25:14-30.

1. Why were the servants given different amounts?

2. What are some of your gifts, and how do you go about using them?

Day 4. The Sower and the Seeds. Mark 4:1-20.

1. What happened when the seeds fell on good soil?

2. Describe what kind of soil your life is today.

Day 5. The Prodigal Son and the Gracious Father. Luke 15:11-32.

1. Why was the older brother angry with his father?

2. Do you see God as your father? Explain.

Day 6. Lazarus and the Rich Man. Luke 16:19-31.

1. Why wasn't Lazarus allowed to give a drop of water to the rich man?

2. Name five people you would like to share the good news with. Pray together for the right opportunities to show God's love.

36 Prayer: *Like Breathing Out and Breathing In*

Adult Reflection

Answer me when I call, O God of my right!
   You gave me room when I was in distress.
   Be gracious to me, and hear my prayer.

Give ear to my words, O LORD;
   give heed to my sighing.
Listen to the sound of my cry,
   my King and my God,
   for to you I pray.
O LORD, in the morning you hear my voice;
   in the morning I plead my case to you, and watch.
   (Psalm 4:1; 5:1-3)

Talking, thinking, giving ourselves over to our Creator is as natural as breathing out and in. Yet we become hindered as we grow up because the trappings of prayer intimidate us. Somewhere along the line we come to believe that there is a formula for prayer. We are taught that it isn't right to pray for this or that. Or that we can't ask unless we have forgiven. Prayer becomes encumbered with rules, etiquette and politics that shut us out and shut us down.

When the disciples said, "Teach us to pray," Jesus taught them a prayer that was meant to free them from the trappings. And his prayer teaches that God is present not just to our words but also to our inarticulate groans, that God cares about our everyday lives and our every need, and that we are given the privilege of approaching without fear and with expectation. We do not need a high priest or a special altar to approach God: God has come within our reach.

I believe one of the reasons God was so delighted with David was that he was so honest in prayer. He was not afraid to be angry, jealous, indignant, humble, childish or poetic with God. In other words, he was his most real when communicating with God. David was also very aware of the necessity of silence in prayer. After all, if you're going to ask, it only makes sense to listen for the answer.

Family Reflection

The people following Jesus asked him to teach them to pray. They didn't know how to pray, because they had always depended on someone they thought was more worthy to pray for them. They were afraid that they would do it wrong. So Jesus taught them a prayer. "God is for you in every way," Jesus taught. "God is to be respected and honored." The one thing about prayer that stands out is that we should just keep at it.

There are lots of ways of praying. We can stand up, sit down, bow our heads, close our eyes, kneel, lift our hands, look at each other, shout, sing, run or be still. The important part is to be real with God. God wants us to be honest with our words, questions and needs. God is always with us.

Day 1. Praying Honestly: The Lord's Prayer. Matthew 6:1-13.

1. What is the difference between a hypocrite's prayer and an honest prayer?

2. When and where do you find yourself praying most often? Why?

Day 2. Keep Knocking. Luke 11:1-13.

1. What does Jesus say is the reason the friend will finally get up and give his neighbor what he needs?

2. Sometimes we carry prayer for someone or something for a long time, even years, and then we might begin to give up. Tell about a prayer you have been praying for a long time, and renew your commitment to keep praying.

Day 3. The Persistent Prayer. Luke 18:1-8.
1. Why did the judge finally rule in favor of the widow?
2. The widow knew that she was right. Do you know of something unfair that is going on in your community or school?
  What kind of prayer commitment are you willing to make?

Day 4. Empty Pride, Empty Words. Luke 18:9-14.
1. Why did the Pharisee consider himself a better person than the tax collector?
  Why didn't Jesus agree with him?
2. What sentence would you use to describe yourself to God?

Day 5. Spirit Prayer. Romans 8:26-27.
1. How does the Spirit help us in prayer?
2. Are you unsure of how or what exactly to pray for? Practice a few moments of silence after you present the situation to God. Your prayer can be as simple as:
  God, here I am again.
  I need a job, I'm not sure how to ask.
    (silence)
Continue this each time you pray, and listen for God's voice.

Day 6. Praying for Our Leaders. 1 Timothy 2:1-7.
1. Why does the author of 1 Timothy encourage us to pray for officials?
2. Find out who your community leaders are, and "adopt" one or two to pray for regularly as a family. At some point you might

drop them a note and let them know your family is praying for them.

Special Activity: Prayer Balloons

For a special treat stop by the grocery store or flower shop and purchase one helium-filled balloon for every member of your family. Pass out slips of paper and pens or markers. Put your prayers on paper. You can draw God a picture or write him a note. Tie the prayers to your helium balloons. In a special celebration of the privilege of prayer go outside together and release your balloons heavenward. Rejoice that God has heard your prayers, and that he cares about you.

(Small children may not want to let their balloon go! That's okay. Just attach the picture or note to your balloon, and let them keep their balloon.)

37 Promises:
Cross My Heart

Adult Reflection

From early childhood we are taught that a promise is something sacred. "Don't make promises you can't keep" is universal advice handed down from generation to generation. Why not? The danger in making promises you can't keep is that soon you will lose the trust of the people who depend on you. We tend not to trust the words of a person who can't or won't back them up with action.

But we can speak confidently of a Creator who always keeps promises. Constancy is one of God's most compelling attributes. Psalms speaks endlessly of God's "faithful" and "steadfast" relationship with us. God's promises are always grander and more comprehensive than anything we could wish for or negotiate. The lame man asks to walk. Jesus forgives his sins, *and* the man walks away carrying his mat.

Some things God never promises. God does not promise us exemption from full participation in life. That full participation involves disappointment, fear, failure, struggle, suffering, grief, jealousy, injustice and temptation. Mixed with joy, peace, contentment, love, passion and victory, these things make up our sacred human story. As you begin to explore the promise-keeping nature of God and the depth of those promises, you will find that God's promises are a solid rock on which to meet the challenges of this life.

Family Reflection

Making promises is a serious business, because people believe us when we make them. Sometimes we keep our promises and other times we don't. Sometimes we have a good reason for not keeping them, and sometimes we really don't have a good reason at all. It bothers us when people break their promises for no good reason.

God's promises are a lot different from ours. God takes promises very seriously; in fact, God has never made a promise that he hasn't kept. God doesn't promise us that life will run smoothly or that things will always be fair. But the promises God makes help us to live our lives the best way we possibly can and to find happiness doing it!

Day 1. Abram Promised a Son. Genesis 15:1-5.
Abram has proven himself an obedient servant to God in his dealings with the King of Sodom.
1. How was God's promise to Abram different from Abram's request?
2. Talk about a time when God's answer to your prayer was much greater than you asked.

Day 2. The Promise of Paradise. Luke 24:39-43.
Jesus has been falsely accused and sentenced to death on the cross. In his final moments he hangs dying between two men who are known criminals.
1. Why does Jesus make a promise of paradise to a criminal?
2. What kinds of things make you feel unworthy of God's promises and keep you from claiming them for yourself?

Think about how the criminal hanging at Jesus' side had the courage to make one request. What request do you have for God today?

Day 3. The Promise of the Holy Spirit. Luke 24:36-49.
Jesus has been crucified and resurrected. He has appeared to the disciples before this, and had a significant conversation with two disciples

on their journey to the nearby town of Emmaus.
1. Why does Jesus want the disciples to remain in Jerusalem?
2. Waiting can seem very difficult at times. Are you waiting for God's direction to help you decide or understand something? What?

Day 4. A Promise for the Entire Household. Acts 2:29-40.
The Holy Spirit has come upon those gathered in Jerusalem on the day of Pentecost. Peter is empowered to come out of hiding and deliver a powerful sermon on the lordship of Jesus Christ.
1. What is required of those seeking God in Jesus?
2. How do we go about claiming this promise for ourselves today?

Day 5. A Promise to Those Who Persevere Through Trials. James 1:12-21.
Crowns or wreaths of leaves or flowers were worn among Jews as symbols of joy and honor at feasts and weddings.
1. To whom has God promised the "crown of life"?
2. What kinds of trials do you find yourself facing today?

Day 6. Magnificent Promises. 1 Peter 1:3-9.
1. Where do the promises of God finally lead us?
2. What promises do you make to God?

38 Repentance:
When Sorry Isn't Enough

Adult Reflection

The children of Israel wandered in the wilderness and cried out for a path leading to the Promised Land. On a swirling mountain, Moses was given the road map. What the Israelites did not understand was that the Promised Land was not just a place to set their tents but a place to set their hearts.

The Ten Commandments were not given just to ensure good behavior and common decency among Abraham's children. They are a window into the character of God and a simple way of understanding our own deepest needs. God has never been in pursuit of our actions as much as God is in pursuit of our entire being.

Throughout history, we have tried to shortchange God by giving good deeds and righteous words without giving too much of ourselves. Cain gave what he thought was required without giving himself, and his jealous heart killed his brother. God blasted the chosen ones when they offered *things* instead of themselves:

Bringing offerings is futile;
　incense is an abomination to me.
New moon and sabbath and calling of convocation—
　I cannot endure solemn assemblies with iniquity.
Your new moons and your appointed festivals
　my soul hates;
they have become a burden to me,
　I am weary of bearing them.
When you stretch out your hands,
　I will hide my eyes from you;
even though you make many prayers,

I will not listen;
  your hands are full of blood. (Isaiah 1:13-15)

These people had become do-gooders, not good-doers. The religious leaders knew all the laws, rules and regulations for living a godly life, but they had forgotten what it means to live a life for God.

True repentance does not stop at changing our behavior. True repentance changes our mind and heart. It's not so much that we will never *do* a particular thing again as that we no longer have the *desire* to do it. We see evil for what it is, and we see it in ourselves. We turn away in the most literal sense from anything that would take us off the path to the Promised Land, and we turn straight into the arms of God.

Family Reflection

What do parents mean when they say, "Sorry isn't enough"? Do they mean you should say, "I'm *very* sorry"? Chances are they want you to understand *why* the thing you have done is unacceptable. But understanding is only the beginning. The next big step is to truly feel, down deep inside, that you would never want to do that again. That isn't easy, and we need God's help. We can pray and ask for God's help. We can ask our family to pray for us, and they will help us also. Not doing something we have been told not to do is a beginning. Not wanting to do it is repentance.

Day 1. Sinner's Prayer of Repentance. Psalm 51:1-17.

1. What are the sacrifices that please God?

2. Name one thing in your life that you feel is not pleasing to God and that you would like to change. Write these concerns in a family journal, and pray regularly for one another. Check in weekly and see how God is working in your life.

Day 2. Zacchaeus Repents. Luke 19:1-10.

1. How does Zacchaeus show he has repented?

2. If Jesus were to come to your house today, what would you want to change about the way you live your life?

Day 3. The Magician Is Urged to Repent. Acts 8:4-24.

1. Why was Simon denied the power to give the Holy Spirit?

2. What are some ways we might try to "buy" or earn a relationship with God?

Day 4. Saul's Conversion and Repentance. Acts 9:1-22.

1. How did other Christians first respond to the news of Saul's conversion?

2. Tell how you came to know Jesus as Savior. Who was surprised by your decision?

Day 5. Repentance Leads to New Creation. 2 Corinthians 5:17-20.

1. As "ambassadors" for Christ, what is our message to the world?

2. With what two persons would you most like to share the good news about Christ's love?

What holds you back from sharing?

Day 6. Thanksgiving for Believers. 1 Thessalonians 1:1-10.

1. What had been the biggest change in the lives of the Thessalonians?

2. What was the most significant change in your life after your decision to accept Jesus as Lord?

39 Salvation:
Driving in Circles

Adult Reflection

Amazing grace, how sweet the sound,
　　That saved a wretch like me.
I once was lost but now am found,
　　was blind but now I see.

As this song so beautifully puts it, were it not for the saving nature of God, not only would we be lost but we would also lack the vision to ever see ourselves home to safety.

There are a million ways to be lost, each as original as the person experiencing it. Those who are quite literally lost may spend hours driving in circles, never reaching their destination. Others are the forgotten ones, who are lost because the compass of their circumstances or the past has trapped them in mental illness, poverty, illiteracy, racism, abuse, violence, injustice. Many of them remain lost because we are blind to them: we cannot or will not see their pain or how our silence keeps the cycle of pain going.

In some way we have all been lost. We put up stumbling blocks between ourselves and God, and we put stumbling blocks in front of others. But God is no lightweight in the warfare for our lives. Jesus' parables speak often about the search for that single lost coin or sheep. God stops at nothing to find us.

Salvation moves and breathes in the way our lives are played out. We cannot be saved and then sit on the shoreline watching others drown. We are called to swim back into the tide with all our strength toward those who are still lost.

Family Reflection

Have you ever felt lost? Maybe you got off a ride at the carnival or stepped off a bus and didn't see the familiar face you were expecting. Just for an instant you felt your heart start pounding and your stomach turn flip-flops. As your eyes raced over the crowd, you finally spotted your parent or friend—the one who made you feel warm and safe and welcome. In fact, you felt saved.

Without God we are lost. Without God we feel afraid and not taken care of, and so we act badly toward each other. God knew how much we needed to be saved. God knew how much we needed to see the face of one who would make us feel warm and safe and welcome. God also knew how hard it is sometimes to understand all of this. So God sent someone who could show us the way and help us understand. God sent someone to save us. God sent Jesus.

Day 1. Jesus Came for Us. Matthew 1:18-23.
1. What was the purpose of Jesus' birth?
2. How has Jesus saved you?

Day 2. God So Loved the World. John 3:16-21.
1. Why do those who do evil hate the light?
2. What kinds of things do you think people try to hide from God?

Day 3. No Other Name. Acts 4:1-12.
Peter and John are speaking the gospel of Jesus Christ boldly. They are witnessing and healing the sick. The religious leaders who were against Jesus now turn their attention to his disciples.
1. According to Peter, how was the lame man healed?
2. In what way does your life need healing?

Name someone you know whose life is troubled. Spend time praying for that person's needs to be met.

Day 4. Everyone Who Calls His Name. Romans 10:1-13.

1. How will we be saved?

2. There are different ways to celebrate when someone accepts Jesus Christ as Lord. How do you celebrate in your church? (For example, does your church use public confession and baptism? Does your church use confirmation?)

Day 5. New Life in Christ. Ephesians 2:4-10.

1. What is a gift?

2. When someone buys a gift for you, who pays for it? What do you owe for receiving this gift?

Day 6. Our Job. 2 Peter 1:3-11.

1. What things are we encouraged to add to our faith?

2. Which of "these virtues" is hardest for you? Why?

Special Activity: Finding Light

In this activity you will discover the wonderful truth that light overcomes darkness. You will need one box (shoebox size or bigger) that has a lid and a match. Show your family the box and the match. Say, "I have a big box of darkness here. I also have one small match. We are going to do an experiment to see which is stronger, darkness or light." Slowly remove the lid from the box of darkness. As you remove the lid, say, "Watch out! I'm letting the darkness out of my box. Does anybody see it?" Hold the box up for everyone to see. Now turn off all the lights in your house. Say, "I'm lighting one tiny little match. Does anyone see the light?"

Discuss the fact that Jesus is the light of the world. Because of Jesus and the gift of salvation we are not lost in the dark anymore. We have been found.

Enjoy candlelight with your evening meal or a special snack. Talk about the joy of knowing the Savior, the Light of the World.

40 Wisdom:
The Heart of the Matter

Adult Reflection

Wisdom is mysterious because it goes beyond knowledge of facts. Wisdom comes from beneath the skin and reaches out to the world and its inhabitants with clarity, sensitivity and keen intuition. Wisdom looks into the heart of a matter and sees the past woven with the present moving toward the future. The wise person has perspective on life.

The words for wisdom in Hebrew and Greek are *hokmah* and *sophia* respectively. *Hokmah* is defined as energy, a divine attribute or energy and the divine wisdom personified. The Septuagint, the Greek translation of the Hebrew Bible, translates *hokmah* as *sophia*. The *Dictionary of the Greek New Testament* defines *sophia* as "wisdom, insight, intelligence, knowledge; Wisdom of God." Both *hokmah* and *sophia* are feminine nouns.

One of the most extensive descriptions of *sophia* in the Protestant canon can be found in Proverbs:

The Lord created me *[Sophia]* at the beginning of his work,
　the first of his acts of long ago.
Ages ago I was set up,
　at the first, before the beginning of the earth. . . .
When he established the heavens, I was there,
　when he drew a circle on the face of the deep, . . .
when he marked out the foundations of the earth,
　then I was beside him, like a master worker;
and I was daily his delight,
　rejoicing before him always,

rejoicing in his inhabited world
   and delighting in the human race. (Proverbs 8:22-23, 27, 29-31)
Paul attributes this wisdom to God:
   For Jews demand signs and Greeks desire wisdom, but we proclaim
   Christ crucified, a stumbling block to Jews and foolishness to Gentiles, but to those who are the called, both Jews and Greeks, Christ
   the power of God and the wisdom *[sophia]* of God. (1 Corinthians
   1:22-24)
Wisdom is most certainly a gift from God.

Family Reflection

My children, Matthew and Sarah, take turns riding in the front
seat when just the three of us are in the car. But sometimes we
skip a few days, and by the time the three of us are in the car
again we have forgotten who sat up front the last time. For a
while this problem started off big arguments, but eventually
Sarah and Matthew showed wisdom in solving the problem.
They decided to be very honest about their memory of who was
last to sit up front. Now if there is a disagreement or nobody
can honestly remember, they both sit in back and start all over
again the next time.

   Wisdom really is very different from being smart or educated.
Wisdom helps you to use what you know to help others. Wisdom helps you see things the way they really are and to understand what makes people do the things they do.

Day 1. Jethro Gives Wise Counsel. Exodus 18:1, 5-9, 13-27.
1. How did Jethro advise Moses to change the way he was
leading the people of Israel?

   Why was Jethro concerned?

2. What person do you most trust to give you wise advice?

   What is the best advice you have ever received?

Day 2. Solomon Judges Wisely. 1 Kings 3.
1. What did Solomon ask from the Lord?
2. If God were to ask you, "What shall I give you?" how would you reply?

Day 3. Commendation of Wisdom. Proverbs 8.
1. What does the person who finds wisdom also find?
2. What would some of the differences be between a president who was smart and a president who was smart *and* wise?

Day 4. The Wisdom of Jesus Is Rejected. Matthew 13:44-58.
1. Why were the people in Jesus' hometown offended by his teachings?
2. Sometimes it's hard to accept advice from those to whom we are closest. If you had just one piece of advice to give one another person about how to have a happy life, what would that advice be?

Day 5. Wisdom Is a Gift of the Spirit. 1 Corinthians 12:1-13.
1. What are the gifts of the Spirit meant to do?
2. Choose a gift that you feel is particularly important and tell why.

Day 6. Wisdom from God. James 3:13-18.
1. What are the characteristics of wisdom from God?
2. Pray together for wisdom to guide your family. Then pray for God's wisdom for all those who hold positions of power in your government and in the governments of the world.

41 Worship: *With Our Heart in Our Hands*

Adult Reflection

Throughout Scriptures worship is set in the context of our need to identify, acknowledge and praise. It is not just that God desires to be worshiped, but that God wishes our need to be met as well. When worship is at its best, we find ourselves approaching God with our heart in our hands. We place it at the feet of God, knowing and believing that it will be received, cherished and nurtured for all eternity. We are not made to feel small and empty in the presence of the Creator. God encourages us to approach with confidence and dignity.

In the assembly of worship we lift our voices in delight, with song and praise. We steal softly into God's presence with prayer and petition. The spoken Word draws us into God's embrace. Rejoicing in all that we have been given, we return a portion. And Christ is so present in the elements of baptism and Communion that a hush falls over us and our voices tremble with emotion.

Yet worship can never be confined or defined by a single act at a single moment. When we are not gathered in formal worship, we act out worship in our attitudes and living styles. We regard our bodies as holy temples and treat them accordingly. It only makes sense that we regard one another in the same manner, and thus peace and health care become issues of worship. We are called to live as worshiping creatures, delighting in the very fact of our creation.

Family Reflection

When something incredibly wonderful happens to us, we want

to dance and sing and smile and laugh! Sometimes people even cry because they are so happy. We want to grab someone's hand and say, "Listen—the most incredible thing! You just won't believe it!" We thank the person who made this wonderful thing possible with a hugs or a phone call or a note.

God made us and the world and everything in it. God wants us to be happy and loved and cared for. God will never leave us alone and will help us through even the tough times. God is good! Don't you think that deserves a celebration? Every Sunday we gather together with our friends and our family for that celebration, and we call it worship. But we can also worship every single day.

Look around you and think about the things you like best and thank God for them. Show kindness to others and thank God for the wonderful people in your life. Give back to your family the love and care you are given. Tell others the incredible news about God's love. These are all ways we worship God. Only God is worthy of worship. No one anyplace or anytime could or would love us so deeply and give us so much.

Day 1. Worship in Daily Living. Exodus 20:1-17.
1. These commandments sum up our responsibilities toward God and toward our neighbors. Which ones are between God and ourselves?

Which ones are between us and our neighbors?
2. Which commandment do you find most difficult to live up to?

Day 2. Commandment for Worship. 1 Chronicles 16:1-13, 23-36.
For more information on the ark of the covenant, read Exodus 25:10-22. The ark was central to the nomadic worshiping community and was

carried on poles by specially appointed men as the Israelites traveled.
1. What were the main jobs of the Levite ministers?
2. List what is included in the order of worship at your church.
Why are these different parts included?
   What is the most meaningful part for you?

Day 3. Worship the Lord. Psalm 96.
1. How is the world to be judged?
2. Take turns saying the thing you love most about God.

Day 4. Satan Tempts Jesus. Matthew 4:1-11.
1. What did all of Jesus' responses to Satan have in common?
2. What tools do you have for resisting temptation?

Day 5. We Are the Temple of God. 1 Corinthians 3:16-17.
1. Traditionally the temple has been thought of as God's dwelling place. How does this Scripture change your understanding of where to find God?
2. In what ways do you take care of God's temple?

Day 6. Jesus Christ Is Lord. Philippians 2:5-11.
1. According to these verses, what two words describe Jesus as a man?
2. What two words would you use to describe yourself, and why?

Part 4
Community Life

42 Environment: *The Rhythm of Life*

Adult Reflection

In Maya Angelou's poem "The Pulse of the Morning," read at the inauguration of President Clinton, we can feel the rhythms of life, the ebb and flow of our world and how we relate to it and to one another. We are given the big picture, and then the road of words narrows to individual responsibility summed up in the poem's simple ending: "Good morning." It is a poem worth reading.

The big picture involves how we as a species love and hate the planet we have been given to exist on. We love it, explore it, paint, write and sing about it. We treasure it in parks and museums. It never ceases to inspire us and move us. Yet we also hate, exploit, pollute, desecrate, mine, chop, drill and suck it dry. We turn our eyes to our own immediate need and act like children without responsibility for now or for later.

Christians must have a deep sense of responsibility for the earth, because we have an intimate knowledge of the Creator of this place. Our intimate knowledge also reveals what is expected of us. How we treat the world is not up to agencies and corporations, it is up to us. Our voice must be heard speaking to those who cannot or will not hear the voice of the wind, the waterfall or the sparrow.

Could this thinking be dismissed as "bleeding heart" ideology? Actually, that is a perfect and poignant description. A heart that bleeds is not frozen or hardened by selfishness and greed. It is a heart filled with compassion and wisdom: enough wisdom to see that we need this earth and we need it in good shape.

Family Reflection

My kids love to go to the beach. We live in San Diego, and that means we can enjoy the beach almost all year round. Some people love to go hiking or camping. Perhaps you like to swim, ride your bike or fly kites.

The earth is an exciting place to live. God made it that way. God also wanted us to take good care of our world. God made each of us responsible to do our part in making sure that happens! But we don't do all the giving. The earth takes care of us as well. Everything we have came from something found in our earth. We rely on the earth for our food, water, shelter and energy. God made us to rely on each other!

Day 1. God Creates Heaven and Earth. Genesis 1:1-13.
1. What did God do to create heaven and earth?
2. What kinds of things can you do to help keep the earth in good condition?

Day 2. God Creates the Sun, Moon, Stars and Animals. Genesis 1:14-25.
1. What commandment was given to the creatures God created?
2. How have we human beings helped God's creatures to do this?

How have we kept them from doing it?

Day 3. God Creates Human Beings. Genesis 1:26-31.
1. How was the creation of human beings different from all other creation?
2. Name two good things about each member of your family.

Day 4. God Destroys Creation Because of Sin. Genesis 7:1-5, 11-12, 15-17, 21-24.
God saw how evil the world had become. There was no goodness to be found among human beings except in Noah, his wife, his sons and

their wives. God decided that the earth must be destroyed to allow a fresh start and instructed Noah on how the new earth would come.

1. Whom did God spare as the world was destroyed? Why?

2. What part of your life would you like to wash away? How would you start again?

Day 5. God Renews the World and Makes a Promise. Genesis 8:20—9:17.

1. A covenant is like an agreement. Who did God make the new covenant with?

2. How does God's covenant make us responsible for all creatures?

Day 6. All of Creation Brings Praise to God. Psalm 148.

1. Why should all of creation praise God?

2. What part of creation do you think is God's most awesome work?

Special Activity: Treasure Hunt

Plan a trip to a favorite outdoor location. A park, seashore, mountain meadow or even your own backyard would work nicely. Each person gets a sack and a list of items that they must find. If your children are quite small, work in pairs. Your list should include one piece of trash and items readily available in the area you have chosen, such as leaves, pods, pine cones, seashells, acorns, dandelions, pebbles. The first person to find everything on the list is the winner of the scavenger hunt.

Once everyone has completed the scavenger hunt, spread your treasures on the ground. Put the pieces of trash on top of the treasures. Discuss how litter makes everything ugly. Before you leave your special place, take time to pick up any litter in the area and put it in your bags to be thrown away later.

43 Justice:
That's Not Fair!

Adult Reflection

> With what shall I come before the Lord,
>   and bow myself before God on high?
> Shall I come before him with burnt offerings,
>   with calves a year old?
> Will the Lord be pleased with thousands of rams,
>   with ten thousands of rivers of oil?
> Shall I give my first born for my transgression,
>   the fruit of my body for the sin of my soul?
> He has told you, O mortal, what is good;
>   and what does the Lord require of you
> but to do justice, and to love kindness,
>   and to walk humbly with your God? (Micah 6:6-8)

Taking care of our neighbors, whether they live next door or around the world, is living justly. As usual, Jesus calls us to a new and radical understanding of our responsibility toward our global family. It isn't enough to take care of one another; we are called to love our neighbor as ourselves. That means more than handing out soup; we are invited to live, feel and walk in our brothers' and sisters' shoes. Walking a mile or two on another's road makes our voice louder and more urgent in calling for equity and fairness.

Jesus says that the second commandment, to love our neighbor, is like the first. Loving each other is a way of loving God. From God's viewpoint, love has never been hearts and flowers. God's love is born out of effort, sweat, commitment, honor, steadfastness and, finally, submission. Submission in its purest form means to put another's best interests before your own. Being fair and just with one another is really a simple matter of passing on what has been so generously given to each of us.

Family Reflection

Whether you are waiting for your turn at tetherball, the snack bar or the bathroom, when you are waiting in line for something, doesn't it seem like it takes forever? And how do you feel when someone bigger than you crowds in front of you in line? Your first thought is probably "That's not fair!" Of course it's not. And that's what justice is all about. The only time justice works is when everyone agrees to play fair. All the people in line behind you know that the fair thing to do is to wait their turn. When people are fair, everyone wins.

But justice isn't just waiting your turn. Justice is also making sure that everyone has a turn. Some people are smaller than you. Some other people think that because they are bigger and stronger, they can push others around. You know this isn't right, but it can be scary to speak up. But what if a whole bunch of you felt the same way? It would only take one person to say, "Hey, let's stand together and make sure they play fair." The problem may not go away, but it becomes easier to work on. God has always been fair with us. Maybe it's time we passed that on to others.

Day 1. What the Lord Requires. Deuteronomy 10:12-22.
The sojourners were those who lived within the covenant community without tribal status. They were the legally helpless and constantly faced the danger of exploitation.
1. In what way is God shown as being impartial?
2. Who live among or near us that might be considered "sojourners"?

Day 2. Joshua Deals Fairly with Rahab. Joshua 2:1-24; 6:20-25.
The children of Israel were on the final leg of their forty-year journey to the Promised Land of Canaan. The city of Jericho stood between

them and the valley leading into Canaan.

1. What promise did Joshua's men make to Rahab?

2. What promises have you made that you are working hard to keep?

Day 3. Justice For God's Beloved. Matthew 5:1-12.

1. According to these verses, to whom does the kingdom of God belong? (See Isaiah 66:2 to learn more about the "poor in spirit.")

2. Choose the beatitude that most fits who you are, and explain why.

Day 4. God's Fairness Becomes Ours. Matthew 7:7-12.

1. How should we treat other people?

2. Describe how you like to be treated. Is it hard to treat others the way you want to be treated?

Day 5. The Laborers in the Vineyard. Matthew 20:1-16.

1. How does the householder justify to the laborers paying the same wages to all?

2. Sometimes justice is hard to take when we feel like we are being shortchanged. Think of an instance when the "fair" thing to do made you feel unhappy. Explain why.

Day 6. Seeing Injustice. Luke 23:33-39.

After being falsely accused by the Jewish religious leaders, Jesus is condemned to die by crucifixion.

1. Why did one criminal feel that Jesus was not being treated justly?

2. Being treated unfairly can be very painful. When have you been treated unfairly? When have you treated someone else unfairly?

44 Poverty:
Not Even a Crumb

Adult Reflection

> Give me a fish and I'll eat today.
> Teach me to fish and I'll eat every day.
> (Mohandas Mahatma Gandhi)

In the past ten years, thanks to global media linkage, we have become eyewitnesses to monstrous poverty. Some of the poor and outcast are forced to rummage through dumpsters, while others are suffering and dying without even garbage to pick through. We see them every day when we drive downtown for dinner or to work. We see them nightly on the news and as we page through magazines.

Yet their poverty is nothing beside the terrible spiritual poverty of those who would deny them food and care because of political principles or pure selfish greed. To turn our backs on the basic needs of those who have been created in God's own image is most certainly to turn our backs on God.

But it's hard to know where to begin to address the problems, and so quite often we do nothing. Many give their money, but fewer give their time and fewer still give of themselves.

In the Scripture study this week is a recurring theme of our responsibility toward our brothers and sisters. God expects us to be involved in one another's lives. Not all in the same way, of course. We are called to diversity and creativity as we enter one another's lives. But we don't have the option of being mere spectators. When we reach over and turn off the needs of others, we ourselves enter the ranks of the spiritually poor. Our poverty comes from a lack of the compassion, mercy and justice to which our Creator calls us.

Family Reflection

The first thing I do after I get up in the morning is to go downstairs and fix the lunches that Sarah and Matthew will take to school with them. They have told me that they want a stretchy fruit snack, not string cheese and crackers. And they ask, "Could I please have two cookies today instead of one?"

I am happy that my kids have these kinds of choices. I am happy that they can go to school with their stomachs full and lunch right around the corner. But I also know that for many people in the world that is not true. I often wonder how I would feel if I had to send my children out without food and nothing for lunch. How would I feel if the weather was cold and they didn't have warm clothes or shoes? How would they feel? How would you feel?

God has made us responsible for one another. That means we are supposed to take care of each other and make sure others have what they need to live. How can you make a difference? This is a very good week to start asking that question.

Day 1. Sharing the Tithe and Caring for the Poor. Deuteronomy 14:28-29; 15:7-11.
1. What was commanded to be given to the poor and needy?
2. What do you consider the five most important things every person must have to live a comfortable life?

Day 2. Responsible for the Poor. Deuteronomy 24:14-22.
1. How were the sojourners, fatherless and widows to be provided for?
2. What does your church do to help the needy?
   How could you do more?

Day 3. The Widow and the Prophet. 1 Kings 17:8-24.
1. The widow had come to the end of her hope. What was she preparing to do when the prophet Elijah met her?

2. Do you know of a place where people are hungry and in trouble? In what way can you make a difference?

Day 4. Prayer for God's Blessings on the King. Psalm 72.
1. How would you describe this king?
2. Do you know of a world leader who is working hard at trying to help the poor and needy? What is he or she doing?

Day 5. The Rich Man and Lazarus. Luke 16:19-31.
1. Why wasn't Lazarus allowed to warn the rich man's family?
2. Perhaps there is someone you see every day who is in need. How can you help that person directly or indirectly?

Day 6. Faith and Works. James 2:1-17.
1. When is faith at a dead end?
2. Do you have stereotypes about the poor who live in your city? How can you learn more about their true circumstances?

Special Activity: Hunger
As you begin your evening meal, without offering any explanation, put on the table only one small bowl of rice and give everyone a cup of water. Listen as your family comments on the meal before them. Are there some complaints? Is anyone surprised? Explain that many people in the world will go to bed tonight having eaten a meal like this one. Discuss the differences between this meal and what your family normally eats. Then, if you wish, go ahead and serve your regular meal. But use the shock of the experience to motivate your family to consider the problem of hunger.

Schedule a time to go to the grocery store and buy canned food for an organization or church that feeds the hungry in your area. If possible, help to serve a meal in a homeless shelter.

45 Service:
Through the Looking Glass

Adult Reflection

When Jesus put the best interest of the person before the law and set the glory of God above all else, the world took a walk through Alice's looking glass where nothing was as it seemed. Through the looking glass of God's incarnation as a human being, we see that "the last shall be first," "the meek shall inherit the earth," "whoever humbles himself like this child is the greatest in the kingdom of heaven," "you also ought to wash one another's feet." We see the Master serving those he would lead. Thus the office of servant takes on new meaning and dignity. Our service to others, then, becomes our service to God. Our understanding of what a privilege it is to serve one another begins to affect the ways we relate to our neighbors both near and far.

Family Reflection

It's an honor to be chosen as a special helper in class, in band or on a team. Sometimes it means extra work, but we don't usually mind because we know that what we are doing is important. We are chosen to serve God in the same way. God gives each of us gifts to share. When we use our gifts to help one another, we are serving God! One of these gifts might be teaching someone something they do not know, like how to play a game or how to work with math problems. Another gift might be encouraging friends when they feel down or listening when they have a problem. There are all kinds of gifts. When we choose to follow the example of Jesus, we are choosing to serve God with our whole heart, cheerfully and with pride.

Day 1. The Great Judgment. Matthew 25:31-46.
1. What did Jesus mean when he said that some did not feed, clothe or take care of him?
2. Talk about how your family is involved in doing the things that Jesus spoke about. How could you do more?

Day 2. Serve Only One Master. Luke 16:10-13.
1. What happens when you try to serve two masters?
2. It's hard to please everyone. Who do you think it is most important to please in your life, and why?

Day 3. Jesus Washes the Disciples' Feet. John 13:1-20.
1. Why were the disciples amazed when Jesus washed their feet?
2. Name three people you think are great leaders. What do you admire most about them?

Day 4. Dorcas Is Raised from the Dead. Acts 9:32-43.
1. How was Dorcas remembered by her neighbors?
2. How do you think you will be remembered by your neighbors?

Day 5. To Live a Godly Life. Romans 12.
1. How are we to overcome evil?
2. Who do you consider to be your enemy?
How could you apply these verses to your relationship with this person?

Day 6. Doers of the Word. James 1:19-26.
1. What does James define as "pure religion"?
2. In what ways are you a "doer of the word"?

46 Sharing:
Just One Word

Adult Reflection

A few years ago Mother Teresa visited San Diego and hosted a large gathering of clergy and lay workers involved in caring for the homeless, sick, neglected and abused. Thousands crowded into a stadium to hear the wisdom and guidance that this small, simple servant of God would share.

Mother Teresa moved to the podium and was asked to address one question: "With so many in need, how can we ever hope to make a difference in the epidemic of hunger and poverty both locally and around the world?" She stood for a long, silent moment, gazing out at the expectant faces, and then spoke just one word, *share.*

Consumer societies enjoy great wealth, yet we continually struggle with poverty in our midst. We must also struggle with an attitude that has shifted many of our "wants" to our "needs" list. How much is enough? We must ask ourselves this question both individually and collectively.

Sharing isn't limited to things. The Bible makes a direct connection between sharing our *things* and sharing our *selves.* When we are able to truly share our selves, the things will follow. As we learn to treasure love more than love our treasure, we become the richest people in the kingdom.

Family Reflection

Imagine that you have a knife. Another person has a loaf of bread, another has peanut butter and a third has jelly. It is way past lunch time, and you are all very hungry. You may stay hungry. The others at least have something to eat, but it is very messy and not too tasty by itself. But what if you all sit down and share? You can all have peanut butter and jelly sandwiches!

Sharing is a funny thing. When you share with someone, you have less left for yourself, but in the end you always have more! How can that be? Well, someone may see you sharing and want to do the same, so they share with you. You may gain a friend or have a good feeling that you didn't have before. If everyone is sharing, then everyone will have plenty.

We really do have plenty to share. It's not just our stuff we need to share, though. We can share ourselves. We can share ourselves with kindness, respect and caring for other people.

Day 1. The Rich Young Man Questions Jesus. Mark 10:1, 13-22.
1. What was this man wanting from Jesus?
2. What things might be standing in the way of your living for God?
How willing are you to get rid of these things?

Day 2. The Widow's Coins. Mark 12:38-44.
1. Why did Jesus consider the widow's gift to be greater than the large sums given by the rich?
2. Discuss how you decide what to give to others. For example, do you give to your church?

Day 3. Ministering Women. Luke 7:37—8:3.
1. In what ways did these women provide for Jesus?
2. Do you know any missionaries? Who supports them with money so that they can continue their work?

Day 4. The Greedy Rich Man. Luke 12:13-21.
1. The rich man had more than he knew what to do with. How did he handle his wealth?
2. What are some ways that people today are doing the same thing as the rich man in this parable?

Day 5. Reap What You Sow. 2 Corinthians 9:6-15.
1. How does God provide for us?
2. In what ways has your family been blessed this year?

Day 6. A Word to Those Who Have the Most. 1 Timothy 6:17-19.
1. How are we to use our riches?
2. What are your hopes for your family's use of money in the future?

Special Activity: Sharing Stuff
It's amazing how quickly "stuff" accumulates. Toys you've outgrown, clothing that is now too small, books that you don't read much anymore—before you know it, closets and cupboards are full with things you rarely use. Take some time to clean out your closets and cupboards. Donate your good, used items to an organization in your area that will put them to use. Maybe the church nursery could use some of your old toys and books. Have fun sharing!

47 Unity:
We Shall Not Be Moved

Adult Reflection

I remember the first time that, as a child, I heard a symphony orchestra play a beautiful piece over the radio. Of course, I could not see what I was hearing, so I asked my mother, "What instrument is making that sound?"

"Which sound?" my mother replied.

"*That* sound," I insisted.

My mother grinned at me and said, "There are many, many instruments making *that* sound!"

This is unity. Every instrument in an orchestra is distinctive in sound, character and style. Were you to listen to each one individually, you would never have any trouble differentiating between the piccolo and the tuba! But when they are assembled under a master's baton with one purpose, their sounds blend as if they were one instrument. Not a single note is compromised nor is a single effort unneeded.

Unity does not mean cloning. Unity is a celebration of differences blending toward a common purpose. Each individual voice, interpretation and conviction is held in high regard. But there is a point when we merge our strengths to stand as one. At this point we know that no forces on earth can move us or shake us from what we must do.

Family Reflection

It's easy to tear a piece of paper. You could probably do it with one hand, a couple of fingers or even your teeth! But what happens when you stack a lot of papers together, like a book or a catalog? If you try to tear the pages, you will find it almost impossible. Do the pages undergo some strange change when they are put together? No, but being together makes them stronger!

The papers may be different colors, weights and sizes, but they all have one thing in common: they tear easily by themselves and become an incredible challenge when put together. This is unity. It's not about being all the same, it's about standing together.

Day 1. The Excellence of Unity. Psalm 133.
1. What is the blessing that the Lord commanded?
2. What kinds of things help your family to enjoy unity?

Day 2. A Kingdom Divided Cannot Stand. Luke 11:14-18.
1. According to Jesus, what happens when people are not united?
2. Tell about a time when your plans were ruined because people could not agree.

Day 3. Different Members of One Body. 1 Corinthians 12:12-26.
1. Which parts of your body seem the least necessary?
2. Choose a member of your family and list three things you consider to be his or her greatest strengths. How do these strengths make a positive difference in your family?

Day 4. Unity of the Spirit. Ephesians 4:1-16.
1. How are we to keep the unity of the Spirit?
2. Why is peace so hard to bring about in our world?

Day 5. Being of One Mind. Philippians 2:1-2.
Paul has reason to believe that the people of the Philippian church are

being divided by petty jealousies. See Philippians 4:2 for more information.

1. How does Paul hope to bring these people back together?
2. What kinds of things divide your family?
   What are some ways you can work on these issues?

Day 6. Putting on the New Nature. Colossians 3:12-17.

1. What binds us all together in perfect harmony?
2. How do we go about "putting on" compassion, kindness, humility, meekness, patience and love?

48 Witness:
Believing, Telling, Living

Adult Reflection

The days following the death of Jesus must have been filled with confusion, panic and fear. The disciples had walked the countryside with Jesus, had seen him perform great miracles and had recently followed him on a triumphal ride into Jerusalem, but then had seen him bleeding on a cross. Now they were left hiding behind shut doors.

When Jesus first appeared to the disciples following his resurrection, Thomas was not with them. Even though it seems apparent that all of the disciples needed physical proof (see John 20:20-21), Thomas's words gained him the dubious title of "Doubting Thomas": "Unless I see the mark of the nails in his hands, and put my finger in the mark of the nails and my hand in his side, I will not believe" (John 20:25).

Is Thomas really so different from you and me? We are constantly in need of reassurance even though we have seen with our own eyes the beauty, strength and grace of God. *Witness* means having personal knowledge and attesting to the truth of what we know. But when that truth is put to the ultimate test, as it was for Thomas and the other disciples, *witness* cannot be separated from *faith*. Our faith becomes our witness and gives meaning to what we have heard and seen. And our lives become the fruit of that witness.

We weren't there to touch the scar on Jesus' side, but we can bear witness to the saving grace of God. We can attest to the truth of what we know by means of our firsthand, personal knowledge.

"Blessed are those who have not seen and yet have come to believe" (John 20:29).

Family Reflection

What you believe about God is part of being a witness. Telling what you believe is another part of being a witness. A third part of being a witness, though, will always end up making the biggest difference. That is taking what we believe and actually living it.

How do we live what we believe? Here is a good example. We believe that God created the earth and everything in it. We read that God liked what was created and said that it was good. We look around and see the beauty of the beaches, mountains and forests, and we are glad. We also believe that God made us responsible for creation. We are supposed to take care of it. Is it enough for us just to tell others that God created the earth and that we are supposed to take care of it? Probably not. What we need to do is take care not to litter, be involved in a recycling program and try not to use products that could harm our environment. When we live our lives the way we believe, that witnesses to what we believe.

Day 1. Daniel Obeys God. Daniel 1:1-16.

The Jews were required to follow very strict food laws. These laws not only were God's commandment but were also a way by which God's chosen race was set apart.

1. Why was the king's servant afraid to do as Daniel asked?

2. In what ways do you honor your body as created by God?

Day 2. Testimony of Jesus. John 5:30-47.

1. What does Jesus say bears witness that he has been sent by God?

2. How can the people you live near, work with or go to school with tell that you are a Christian?

Day 3. Peter Gives Testimony. Acts 10:34-43.

1. What commandment was given to the witnesses of Jesus?

2. What do you believe that God expects of you?
How do you go about doing what is expected?

Day 4. Paul at Corinth. Acts 18:1-11.

1. What did Paul do when the Jews rejected his teachings about Jesus?

2. What is the most frustrating thing about sharing your beliefs?

Day 5. A Life Worthy of the Lord. Colossians 1:1-14.

1. What did Paul say he and Timothy did after hearing about the faith of the people in Colossae?

2. Even today some Christians struggle for their lives and for their faith. Discuss a situation, whether local or global, where Christians are struggling. Agree to pray for them regularly.

Day 6. Paul Lives as a Witness. 2 Timothy 4:1-7.

1. Why did Paul feel content to die?

2. What are some things that you feel are important to accomplish before you die?

Part 5
Celebrating the Seasons

49 Christmas: *Why Not a King?*

Adult Reflection

The world waited. All of creation had once been swallowed in a great flood. Fatted calves, pigeons, doves and lambs were now offered regularly to prove that the heart of humanity did not belong to things but to God. What price would be demanded next? Who could know? But it would be something grand, you could be sure. Something or someone glorious and marvelous would come as God's ambassador. A king! Why not a king?

Into our cold, dark, silent winter world came a small, fragile cry. It was the cry of new life gasping for air—of untried lungs filling with the fragrance of hay, animals and Mother. The silence was shattered as a thousand angels sang their lullaby of joy to the newborn in Bethlehem. The shepherds felt the mystery of hope filling the night and began to move quickly toward the presence of God. Trembling excitement raced through the hills on the feet of all those who sought to be the first to see the living miracle. Was this the king?

Family Reflection

God had to come up with a great plan. The whole world was waiting. Hundreds of years before, people called prophets had said that God would send someone to show us how to be close to God. Most people expected God to send a great king. After all, people had only seen God as a pillar of fire or a burning bush before. Who better to speak for God than a majestic king with a huge army? But guess what—God had a different plan, a plan that took everyone by surprise. So on a cold winter night God came to earth as a baby! God came as Jesus. When we celebrate Christmas, we aren't just celebrating the birth of Jesus. We are celebrating God's wonderful plan.

Day 1. Birth of John the Baptist Foretold. Luke 1:5-25.
1. What made the news about Elizabeth's pregnancy so unusual?
2. Elizabeth had waited a long time for her prayers for a child to be answered. She had given up on the possibility. Tell what you have prayed for the longest. Don't give up! With God nothing is impossible.

Day 2. Birth of Jesus Foretold. Luke 1:26-38.
1. What was Mary's reaction to what the angel told her?
2. What was the most incredible news you have ever received? How did you feel when you heard it?

Day 3. Mary Visits Elizabeth. Luke 1:39-56.
1. What happened when Mary visited Elizabeth?
2. Whom do you go to when you want to share important things that are happening? Why?

Day 4. John Is Born. Luke 1:57-80.
1. What did John's father, Zechariah, prophesy about the plan God had for John?
2. Talk about the gifts that you think God has given your different family members. How could these gifts be used to spread God's love in the world?

Day 5. Jesus Is Born in Bethlehem. Luke 2:1-20.
1. How did the shepherds know that Jesus was the Savior?

2. Tell about how you came to know Jesus as Savior.

Day 6. Jesus Is Presented at the Temple. Luke 2:21-38.
1. What did Simeon and Anna have in common?
2. What elderly people are important to you?
   How can you show them that you care today?

Special Activity: Christmas Ornaments
Spend an evening making some simple decorations for your Christmas tree. You can use construction paper, glitter and ribbon, or cookie dough and frosting to create some unique ornaments. Here are some ideas: a crown with "King Jesus" on it, a globe with a bandage strip that says "Jesus" on it, a pretty package that says "Jesus, God's Greatest Gift," or a birthday cake that says "Happy Birthday, Jesus."

50 Easter:
The Road Home

Adult Reflection

No matter how the season is commercialized, the truth of that first Easter morning cannot be covered up. The evidence is sometimes hidden when our vision is narrowed to only our own struggles and situations, but the victory still exists! The resurrection is not just our story of triumph over death. It is the story of God's persistent pursuit of grace into the darkest corners of our lives, even when that pursuit winds into the belly of Sheol. It is the evidence of the value of human beings. God made us worthy, and in God's death in Jesus we are lifted up. The resurrection lifts us up with hope and promise.

The resurrection is a confirmation of Christmas. Into this world God came humbly with vulnerability and nakedness. And only one thing is humbler than birth: death. Jesus did die. But out of the tomb came the Christmas promise kept—the promise that forevermore we have a road home. This is a promise that we can make it no matter what obstacles lie in the road. This is a promise that we need never journey alone. Even as we draw our last earthly breath, there waits for us the wonder of rebirth and the gift of an eternity with the Lord.

Family Reflection

Spring is a celebration of new life. In the spring animals give birth to their young, flowers bloom and snow melts. There could be no new life for us without Easter. God wanted to bring us close so that we would live in God's presence forever when we were finished here on earth. God did this by giving us Jesus, who died on the cross and then came back to life! This showed us that nothing could separate us from God, not even death.

Day 1. Jesus Enters Jerusalem. Matthew 21:1-17.
1. Who did the crowds say Jesus was?
2. How do you describe Jesus to others?

Day 2. Jesus Is Anointed: The Last Supper. Matthew 26:1-25.
1. Why did Jesus say the woman who poured oil on his feet had done a "beautiful thing"?
2. What is the very best thing you can offer to God?

Day 3. Gethsemane: Judas Betrays Jesus. Matthew 26:30-56.
1. Which disciples stayed with Jesus?
2. Can you remember a time when you were too frightened to do what you knew was the right thing?

Day 4. Jesus Before Pilate. Matthew 27:1-31.
1. Why did Pilate try to convince the crowd to ask for Jesus' release?
  Why did he give in to the crowd's demands?
2. How does your crowd influence the way you make decisions?

Day 5. The Death and Burial of Jesus. Matthew 27:32-66.
1. What did Jesus cry out as his last words?
2. Have you ever felt as though God had left you? What was it like?

Day 6. The Resurrection of Jesus. Matthew 28:1-20.
1. The women saw Jesus and worshiped him. What happened when the disciples saw him?
2. How do you celebrate the story of Jesus' resurrection?

Special Activity: Egg Promises

Hard boil plenty of eggs and provide every member of your family with a crayon. On each egg draw a picture reminding you of the Christmas promise, and a picture reminding you that the promise has been kept through the victory of Easter. For example, you could draw a manger and a cross, a baby and a king, a stable and an empty tomb. After you have drawn pictures on the eggs, dye the eggs any bright colors you choose. Dye will not adhere to the crayon, and your pictures will be visible reminders of the fact that God keeps his promises and Jesus is alive.

51 Pentecost:
The Church Is Born

Adult Reflection

What would it take to lay all doubts to rest? What would it take to bring the apostles and other disciples out of the closets where they were hiding and trust the truth of what they had seen and heard?

We are told that at the Feast of Pentecost thousands gathered in Jerusalem to celebrate the giving of the law. What were they seeking? They were foremost longing for God's promises to be kept. Perhaps they were also seeking a safe place to worship with opened eyes in the comfort of community.

In the ancient images of wind and fire God's presence came sweeping into their midst. The Spirit of God was poured out and filled the lives of everyone present. The travail experienced on the cross and the passage out of the tomb gave way to the glorious birth of Christ's church.

Family Reflection

So much had happened to the disciples of Jesus! The one they thought was God's chosen king had been crucified, but they had seen him again. Still, they were very afraid that they would be the next ones killed, and so they were hiding. But Jesus had told them to go to Jerusalem and to wait for the Holy Spirit, and that was just what they did.

God always keeps promises. In a wonderful experience the Spirit of God came to be with all the people waiting in Jerusalem. They weren't afraid anymore! They could understand one another. They felt like a family. They knew exactly what they needed to do, and they felt brave enough to do it! And so the church was born.

Day 1. Jesus Instructs the Apostles. Acts 1:1-11.
1. What did the apostles expect from Jesus?
   What did Jesus expect from his apostles?
2. What do you expect from God?
   What do you think God expects from you?

Day 2. Judas's Death: Matthias Is Selected. Acts 1:12-26.
1. What were the requirements for becoming one of the apostles?
2. How can we be witnesses for Christ without actually seeing the events of his life?

Day 3. The Day of Pentecost. Acts 2:1-24.
Jewish tradition held that the Law was given on this day, seven weeks after Passover.
1. What was the message Peter had for those who did not believe?
2. What message do you have for those who do not believe?

Day 4. The Church's Beginning. Acts 2:36-47.
1. How were the daily lives of those first believers changed?
2. How does being a Christian change the way you live every day?

Day 5. Peter and John Are Arrested. Acts 4:13-23.
Peter and John have been arrested by the Jewish religious leaders for healing in the name of Jesus and preaching his resurrection.
1. Why did the religious leaders want Peter and John to keep silent?

2. What things keep you from sharing your experiences as a Christian?

Day 6. The Church Community. Acts 4:32-37.
1. How did members of the early church take care of one another?
2. How do the people in your church take care of each other?

Special Activity: Pentecost Party
Have a Pentecost Party to celebrate the birthday of the church. You could invite your pastor or other church leaders to celebrate with you if you like. Serve birthday cake and sing happy birthday to the church. Give your church a gift, such as food for the pantry, cleaning supplies, office supplies or even a day of labor to do whatever is needed. Thank God for the marvelous gift of the Holy Spirit and the church.

52 Thanksgiving:
Bounty and Blessings

Adult Reflection

Our American tradition of gathering friends and family and sharing a feast is a celebration of the hopes and dreams of the first Thanksgiving being realized. In the cold, severe winter of that first settlement in the New World, the hearts of those present were warmed by the promise of a bountiful future and the blessings of newfound friends. In the midst of an intense struggle between the harshness of an unsettled land and a pioneer spirit, a moment was found to lay aside the thoughts of bone-weary labor and count one's blessings.

Even though a formal Thanksgiving isn't celebrated in all countries, humankind has observed some kind of custom of giving thanks since the beginning of time. We are compelled to turn our hearts and uplifted arms toward God in worship, praise and gratitude. And the grace of God, which receives us so warmly, fills the cornucopia of human need and blesses us beyond measure.

Family Reflection

It's hard to believe that right in the middle of really hard times you can stop and count all the good things happening as well. That is exactly what the people at the first American Thanksgiving feast did! The winter had been very hard. They had worked and worked and worked just to survive and the future looked pretty uncertain. But in the middle of all this they had plenty to celebrate. After all, they had made it so far, and they had the Native Americans as friends. God gives the world so much that God's people have to stop and say thank you sometimes. It's fun to count your blessings—you may be surprised where they will pop up!

Day 1. The Lord's Goodness. Psalm 111.
1. What are at least five things for which the psalmist is thankful?
2. What are five things for which you are thankful?

Day 2. Hymn of Praise. Psalm 147:1-8.
1. How does the psalmist recognize the compassion of God?
2. In what ways has God helped to heal you when you were deeply hurt?

Day 3. The King's Dream Is Revealed. Daniel 2:12-23.
Daniel and his friends have been appointed as wise men of office in the king's palace even though they are captives from Israel. The king feels betrayed by the wise men in his court and has called their bluff by demanding that they tell him what he has dreamed rather than interpreting his dream. This proves to be an impossible task for all.
1. How was Daniel able to know what the king had dreamed?
2. In what ways do you include God in your difficult decisions?

Day 4. Paul Is Thankful in Prison. Philippians 1:1-14.
Paul is under military guard but has managed to witness to even the guards!
1. How did Paul use his situation to continue his work for the Lord?
2. How can you use the situation you are in—at school, home or work—to serve the Lord?

Day 5. Encouragement For Christian Living. 1 Thessalonians 5:12-28.

1. How are we to treat the people with whom we serve the Lord?

2. Name one person with whom you feel especially impatient. Talk about ways that you might improve your attitude toward this person.

Day 6. Prayers of the Redeemed. Revelation 6:9-17.

1. Who were the people in the vision?

2. What is it about God for which you are most grateful?

Special Activity: Popping Blessings

You will need lots of balloons and small pieces of paper. Every day during the week, each family member should write at least one thing that he or she is thankful for on a piece of paper and fold the paper up so that it is very small. Put the paper inside a balloon. On Thanksgiving day blow up all the balloons that you have accumulated during the week and use them as decorations. Conclude your day by playing "Popping Blessings." In relay fashion, take turns popping the balloons, reading the paper inside and shouting out, "Thank you God for *[whatever the paper says]!*" The first team to pop their share of the balloons wins.

Using the *Topical Family Bible Companion* in Your Church

Why use the *Topical Family Bible Companion* as a churchwide program? The goal of the book is to aid in establishing a routine of study that works for busy people. The program is set up to be done in the home, normally requiring ten- to fifteen-minute blocks of time. Either of these make an excellent follow-up for those families whose children have been presented with gift Bibles from the church. They are also great gifts for new members and for children who are baptized.

How Do We Get Started?
First, present the book to your education committee. Make sure this program will be supported by the committee and church staff. Then recruit a leader or leaders who have a sincere love for the Bible and a desire to see others grow in the knowledge and understanding of God's Word. The leader will be responsible for organizing and implementing the reading program.

You may want to introduce the book to the rest of the congregation during Sunday-morning worship. A program that fosters regular Bible study is in keeping with the spirit of worship. This also allows the congregation to be affirmed by the support of the church staff.

How Do We Tell Them?
Begin your publicity with an article in your church newsletter. The Sunday the program is presented from the pulpit, a registration insert could be included in your bulletin. A flyer with an attached registration sheet can be sent home with all Sunday-school students. Use any source of communication (bulletins, information sheets, and so on) that is available to you and reaches your broadest constituency. Remember, word-of-mouth is always the most effective publicity.

How Do We Keep Track?
Have a centralized location (booth or table) where the registration forms can be turned in. Two Sundays are recommended for registration. A large banner or sign on or near your registration locale is helpful in directing people for registration turn-in/pick-up. Have a sample book available plus extra registration forms. The primary source of registrations will probably come from your bulletin insert and Sunday-school flyer.

Once registration is complete, you'll know how many copies to order from your local Christian bookstore. Get the books into the hands of those who signed up as soon as possible to keep the momentum high.

How Do We Follow Up?
To help people stay on track, you might want to arrange a follow-up program to encourage families through the year. This could be done through phone-calling, church-wide progress charts or quarterly parents' meetings.